# TABLE O

# COPS AND ROBBERS

## THE PAST, THE PRESENT, AND THE FUTURE

BY

DAWN WILLIAMS FERREIRA, PH.D.

JINHO "THE PIPER" FERREIRA

**ISBN** 978-0-9915334-0-4

www.pipedreamzent.com

We dedicate this book to our ancestors,
our families,
our teachers,
our students,
our community's protectors,
and those who strive to be a bridge for the children to cross.

The time is now.

# ACKNOWLEDGEMENTS

Ami Zins and Lew Levinson for the hours upon hours of pure dedication to the project. It seems like yesterday I knocked on your door with play in hand. We transformed your living room into a theater, kept the neighbors up, and tried not to knock over any furniture. It's been one heaven of an experience, thank you both for everything.

All of the volunteers that made the *Cops and Robbers* show possible. You all came out because you believed in the message. You beautiful people give us the fuel to continue.

Jim Dennis Photography for the Character Backstory photos, video shoot photos, and all of the shows you have attended.  Your action shots always capture the spirit of what's at hand.

Meres-Sia Gabri El for your book editing, poignant insight, and constant encouragement.  We appreciate your eyes and your heart in this project.

James Farr for staying up 24 hours a day/7 days a week. From the book, to the EP, to the stage play to whatever else I may have dreamt up. When I called you answered, and that's worth more than a lot.

Ed Bantlow for your organizational excellence, 10 emails a day, and solution-focused methods. We'll be doing something great sooner than you know it.

Geoffrey Godfrey for taking time away from your war to come help out with mine. We lost more than we could handle, but gained more than we could imagine.

Adimu for "Throwing the rope," Nedra for showing the way, and Carolyn for phenomenal costume design.

Hodari Davis you raised us to be pit bulls with the art. I'm sure you're not surprised by any of this. Thank you for always being there.

Marty Neideffer for believing in what the world said was impossible and for taking action when it would have been easier to do nothing.

Reto Peter, Dave López, and Arion Salazar for contributing to another fresh musical creation. We're just getting warmed up!

Beli Sullivan for your excellence in video editing; Martin Hoang for being a graphic designer extraordinaire; Ayesha Walker for the West Oakland photos and behind-the-scenes shots. Traci Lee and Taninha Ferreira for your assistance with book formatting and countless volunteer hours; Anthony Moncado and Sandy Berkowitz for believing. This is a huge project with many moving parts. It absolutely took a village to complete it.

Dr. Fred and Nessie Williams, thank you for modeling the intense labor, perseverance, and balance it takes to work together as a couple to complete a project.

The Oakland Rotary Club, 32Ten Studios, Oakland-California Youth Outreach, YGB, and Sound Wave Studios. Thank you for your support.

We could literally fill every page of this book with acknowledgements and still not include some of the people most important to this project. For this reason we intentionally kept the acknowledgements short. If you do not see your name or organization, just know that your support has inspired us to fight full speed ahead and together we will change the world.

# INTRODUCTION

It is with sincere love that we have written this book. Love for our community, love for our family, and love for each other. This collaborative effort is written by a couple that came of age in the 1990's. Jinho is an artist and a law enforcement officer. Dawn is an educator and an advocate for mental health. We are the parents of two sons and one daughter, but we see our roles as protecting and educating our community's sons and daughters as well as our own.

Jinho has a degree in Black Studies and with his band Flipsyde, he has toured the world performing in front of audiences of every hue. This speaks to how knowledge of self can be a source of unification and not necessarily isolation. We know that we are not a post-racial society but we also know that people of African descent have opportunities that they did not have at one time in United States history. We view many of the problems in the black community as resolvable by only black people. This includes but is not limited to the images that we project of ourselves; how we define Blackness; how we will collectively heal from the wounds of slavery, what Dr. Joy De Gruy terms Post-Traumatic Slave Syndrome; how we as a people value our own lives; and how we create our own destinies. We feel that we, as black people, should hold ourselves accountable for our actions, just as we should hold mainstream America, the private business sector, and the government responsible for the ways that they can negatively impact our community. We see the government and all of its institutions as responsible for being antiracist entities that welcome, invite, and allow all historically oppressed people to hold power, be a part of the solution, and contribute to defining reality.

We wrote this book together because we wanted to tell the backstory for Jinho's one-man play *Cops and Robbers*, a look at the dysfunctional relationship between the media, law enforcement, and the black community. In order to convey the full narrative, we realized that, like the play, we would have to provide an historical context for the present day realities.  Our book moves from a chronicled essay to our personal story.

In the first chapter, we compile a history of law enforcement and the black community.  We draw from a history of white policing of enslaved Africans and discuss how the black community could be at odds with the police as enforcers of laws that were meant to subjugate.  We briefly explore the relationship between hip-hop culture and the police.

Chapters two, three, and four unravel the mystery of how a hip-hop artist became a public safety officer in more of a memoir-style. We disclose some of the conversations and epiphanies that we have had as professionals in our fields of expertise. Chapter four is also where readers will find the script for Piper's *Cops and Robbers* and notes on the development of the characters in the play.

The fifth chapter delves into potential improvements that can be made to the current system. We take a look at how shifts have begun to occur and how they can advance with a change in mind state.

Finally, the book closes with Dawn's curriculum, which can assist teachers and parents in processing *Cops and Robbers* with students and youth. These lessons take into account possible triggers from the play and the mental health of the audience.

This book is not an anti-cop diatribe nor is this a plug for the unconditional acceptance of all police officers. Our message is simple and it is the same message that Flipsyde has been promulgating since its inception: **examine multiple perspectives in seeking the truth.** If all of us can put our best effort forward and put more focus on solutions than on our differences, we can transcend and evolve. This book is for open-minded and forward-thinking individuals. We challenge our readers to think about the complexities of race, look critically at mainstream media, and imagine the possibilities in the future of public safety. We hope that this book sparks productive action.

*Jinho & Dawn Ferreira*

## ONE

# A BRIEF HISTORY OF LAW ENFORCEMENT AND THE BLACK COMMUNITY

The title of this book and the play, *Cops and Robbers,* evokes the image of a childhood game, an awareness of "good" versus "evil," and the power that a gun represents in either set of hands. In this game, law enforcement is characterized as a force of morally correct individuals, while robbers are the bad criminals. Opposing the police would seem unacceptable to some.  However, the historical relationship between law enforcement and black America shows that there has been a conflicting sense of what is right and what is wrong. Opposition to law enforcement has deep cultural roots in the black community, and a look into American history may explain why.

For the first 345 years of African presence in what is now known as the United States of America, black interactions with the criminal justice system almost completely revolved around laws meant to subjugate, disenfranchise, and control. The government passed Slave Codes as early as 1650, which were enforceable by all whites against all Africans. This meant that *all* whites, as far as Africans were concerned, were law enforcement officers (Dulaney, 1996). Crimes enforced against Africans during this period included:

1. Learning to read
2. Teaching others to read
3. Attempting to achieve freedom
4. Aiding others in achieving freedom
5. Raising a hand against any white person (even in self-defense)
6. Owning weapons
7. Assembling (thought to be a space for planning uprisings)
8. Being rebellious (i.e. testifying against white people, refusing to work for free, protesting rape or sexual assault)

Intelligence, bravery, self-sacrifice, self-defense, and a desire to achieve freedom described the characteristics of a black "criminal." These traits directly contradicted the profile of an African that mainstream American society desired most: docile, ignorant, complacent, obedient, and sub-human. Snitching meant aiding the authorities in capturing that "criminal," who would in-turn be sentenced to hundreds of lashes, sold away from his or her family, or beaten to death.

Even as black people took action toward self-sufficiency, their efforts were thwarted when their presence pushed the boundaries on the spaces that whites wanted them to occupy. Southern plantations could be characterized as small oppressive territories, and transitioning out of slavery was similar to immigration. The resilience, self-determination, and enthusiasm to succeed during the Reconstruction era were palpable amongst former slaves. In fact, three years after slavery ended, Africans had secured the majority of the South Carolina State Legislature. In the years that followed blacks elected two Senators in Mississippi and a governor in Louisiana. In addition, black people built their own communities, started businesses, founded schools, ran their own newspapers, and policed their own communities. Dulaney (1996) showed that in many black-policed areas the arrest rates of blacks mirrored their population. In several Southern states African American police officers also had the authority to arrest white people, which was widely protested by white civilians. Some frustrated whites organized terrorist groups, like the Ku Klux Klan.

After eleven years, the Hayes Tilden Compromise reversed many of the gains black people made during Reconstruction (Blackmon, 2008). Southern whites, with a vengeance from losing the Civil War, created a hostile, "anti-black" climate that rang with jealousy of the tremendous amount of progress black people made in such a short amount of time. Law enforcement, in the form of Union troops that had been placed in the South to protect blacks from terrorist groups, were withdrawn and returned to the north. Authorities turned a blind eye as Southern whites usurped blacks' newly found political power. Black police officers became the object of police brutality (Dulaney, 1996) and were replaced with local law enforcement comprised mostly of poor whites, often members of terrorist organizations.

Black Codes were enacted throughout the South to decrease black power. These codes prevented Africans from testifying against any white person, serving on a jury or militia, or expressing political concern publicly. Black Codes were also a way of returning blacks to work for very little pay, and in most cases none at all. Black Codes forced Africans to sign annual employment contracts, marrying their cheap labor to a wealthy landowner's plantation.  Africans refusing to sign employment contracts would eventually be found in violation of vagrancy laws and arrested. Bail would be set outside of their ability to pay, wealthy landowners would pay it, and the African would end up working that landowner's plantation until the debt was paid.  Should an African run away from his labor contract, he would be labeled a "fugitive of labor," arrested, and returned to his place of "employment."

White terrorist groups rode throughout the South murdering and intimidating any African guilty of attempting to vote, or encouraging others to do so. The black criminal profile characteristics at this time included self-respect, a will to seek justice and political power, a desire to be economically free, and an attempt to rebel against mainstream America's expectations for Africans. All whites had the power to enforce the Black Codes against all Africans. For many in the black community, all whites were considered to be law enforcement.

As the Supreme Court continued its onslaught against Africans; with *Dred Scott v. Sandford* in 1857, Civil Rights Cases in 1883, and *Plessy v. Ferguson* in 1896, an American apartheid was established. The enforcement of Jim Crow laws demanded that Blacks seclude themselves to a second-class citizenship status. In *Plessy*, the Supreme Court ruled whites and blacks would have separate facilities in everything, and as long as the facilities were equal, this ruling was constitutional. However, in researching this decision, it is nearly impossible to find instances in which real equality mirrored legislated equality. All whites had the power to enforce Jim Crow laws against all Africans within the jurisdictions governed by those laws. Once again, all whites were considered law enforcement.

Throughout the Civil Rights Movement, the public saw images of non-violent, intelligent, proud, courageous, and self-sacrificing blacks targeted with water hoses, dogs, and jail because they fought to achieve real equality. Part of the mentality of the time was that when black people collectively went against the law, they had to craft their movements with precision and detail because scrutiny would ensue. This led to the NAACP's selection of Rosa Parks to begin the Montgomery Bus Boycott instead of Claudette Colvin, an unwed teen mother who was arrested nine months before Parks for not giving up her seat to a white woman. The Civil Rights rebellion was largely led by religious leaders, namely Baptist preacher Martin Luther King, Jr. and the Nation of Islam's Malcolm X, who personified two different black philosophies. Many African Americans resonated with King's philosophy of forgiveness and sought to unify with whites in making demands on a human level. Other black people related to X's sense of self-determination and wanted to see "separate but equal" realized.

The Black Panther Party for Self-Defense continued to vigorously mobilize people where the Civil Rights Movement left off. Founded by two college students, the secular organization appealed to people of different affiliations, various education levels, and socio-economic backgrounds. With an aggressive, unapologetic style, the Panthers' demands included access to jobs, food, housing, decent education, and an end to police brutality. Racial profiling and the inequitable policing practices of law enforcement officers who were sometimes members of the Ku Klux Klan (Chalmers, 1981), motivated the Black Panthers to study the law, police the police, and carry weapons. Racist cops became the iconic "pigs" and compliance with the police, or being an informant, meant selling out the entire race.

One of the founding members of the Black Panther Party, Huey Newton, in his autobiography *Revolutionary Suicide* (1973), sums up the idea of snitching. He shares a time when his classmates encircled him and beat him up. Though someone had called the police, Newton refused to cooperate. In his words,

> I did not want to be an informer because this was a problem
> between the brothers; the outside racist authorities had nothing

to do with it. I have always believed that to inform on someone to the teacher, the principal, and the police was wrong.  These people represent another world, another racial group.  To be white is to have power and authority, and for a Black to say anything to them is a betrayal.  So I did not inform, and they escaped the police; but they could not escape me. (p.46)

Newton places black unity first, joining desegregated schools with the typical view of law enforcement as an outside force. He continues to describe how he armed himself with a pistol and a hammer and physically struck back against his foe.  In this way, black-on-black crime can in some cases be seen as vigilantism, or taking matters into one's own hands.

The community-minded, vigilant, and politicized Black Panther Party was transformed over time into ruthless street gangs with dismal political interests becoming as Mike Davis describes "the bastard offspring of the Panthers' former charisma." COINTELPRO was the most significant purveyor of the dismantling of the Black Panther Party. In addition, the loss of blue-collar jobs, the infiltration of crack, and the War on Drugs disfigured the black community. Michelle Alexander's book *A New Jim Crow* is a necessary read for anyone interested in the effects the War on Drugs has had on black America. In short, she is saying there are so many black people tied up in the criminal justice system, that if the War on Drugs is not an intentional attack on African Americans, it could easily be mistaken for one. With nearly one in three black males between the ages of 20 and 29 caught in the web of the criminal justice system, and the highly publicized incidents of police brutality throughout the United States, black people have little reason to believe anything has changed in their relationship with law enforcement.

## Hip-hop and Law Enforcement

No other music has illustrated the black community's disgust with law enforcement better than hip-hop. Hip-hop culture and law enforcement could be seen as polar opposites. Philosophically, hip-hop is black. Law enforcement is white. Hip-hop is creativity, freedom, and spontaneity. Law enforcement is uniformity, boundaries, and strategizing.

Since its inception, hip-hop music has been the soundtrack of the oppressed. Hip-hop is the proverbial child of the Black Panther Party that gave permission to critique the system with a bold and direct style. These predominately black, male voices have been a monumental expression of creativity originating from artists speaking truth to power, teaching history lessons, and narrating life experiences. This has meant that the law-abiding African American who was racially profiled, the college athlete, the pimp, and the drug dealer could all relate to anti-cop sentiments in the music. There is also a crucial element of boasting which comes from being the survivors of enslaved ancestors. Hip-hop artists poetically brag about their wealth, women, and weapons because they are assertions of a power that has historically been taken away.

Today this power translates into the oppression of others and the glamorization of materialism, which becomes attractive to a diverse audience. Diverting from the original roots of hip-hop, the music has become more reflective of a drug culture that has driven money over morals and then sometimes dropped dollars back into the community.

Many conscious rappers tend to dislike the police because of the historical racism that cops represent. Many gangster rappers tend to dislike the police because law enforcement officers embody an opposition to a criminal lifestyle that these artists either participate in or act like they do. However, some of these hip-hop artists made songs about hating cops and then played them in Hollywood. While maintaining their hip-hop image, their fictional portrayals rewrote the script on what a cop could be. To know the history of law enforcement and the role that rap plays in actively speaking out against the police, it would seem unheard of for a rapper to actually become a *real* cop. Yet, there is one hip-hop artist who seems to have made sense of it all. He is "The Piper."

## TWO

# WHO IS THE "PIPER"?

Born with a name that most find too difficult to pronounce, a face that few forget, a creative mind that blows people away, and the power to communicate and see different perspectives, my husband makes people think.  Jinho Ferreira, also known as the artist Piper, is a beautiful and complex man from West Oakland who is constantly evolving.

When Piper was seven, his mother divorced his Brazilian father.  As the man of the house, Piper constantly had the safety of his loved ones in mind. On several occasions, Piper found himself poised to avenge disrespectful acts toward his family but found that his verbal skills worked effectively. Being a protector, an observer, and a communicator would prove useful in years to come.

Piper's first teacher was his mother, lovingly referred to as Mama, who knew that knowledge of self was paramount. Her collection of black movies, documentaries, and books challenges the West Oakland Library's. An avid reader of history books and detective novels, Mama was determined to make sure Piper was a reader, even if that meant paying him to read. She would write the names of all of her children in each book she owned, recognizing that the knowledge gained was to be shared amongst the family. Mama grew up at a time when her community college education made her more educated than many of her colleagues at the company where she worked. Her self-awareness pushed her to fight for equal pay as a black woman working for a large corporation. As a witness in a case where accusations of racism against the company were raised, a lawyer once facetiously asked her if she was an expert on racism. Her response, shined of her wit and candor, when she said, "Yes, because I am a black woman who was born in 1944, and I have more experience with race relations than anybody in this courtroom."

Mama had seen her neighborhood in West Oakland change from a place where she could leave her children with her neighbor to a place where her neighbor was pimping under-aged girls. The gunshots, the disrespect, and the negativity toward black people were coming from black people. Mama battled against drug dealers consistently hopping her fence and using her backyard as an escape route from police.  After asking on numerous occasions that these youngsters respect her property and them not complying, she placed a strip of spikes on the top of her fence. Mama recounts silently laughing in pleasure while listening to the screams of fleeing street thugs who had attempted to climb her fence in the dark.

As a single mother, raising a black boy during the crack epidemic presented a challenge.  Teenagers standing on the corner were making thousands of dollars a day selling drugs and were recruiting from Piper's age group constantly.  Mama made sure that Piper always had money in his pockets.  She was concerned and saw her son as potential prey for the thug lifestyle. Mama was equally worried about the cops riding around her community, mistaking Piper for one of these drug dealers.  Her greatest weapons against racism, materialism, and self-hatred were knowledge of self, faith, and love.

Seeing his mother prepare and organize a household, go to work on time each day, rarely call in sick, budget her income, and provide for her family taught him early lessons on responsibility. All of her children graduated from college because she showed them the importance of education.

Piper's mother was not big on discipline. She was busy providing for her family and she was not always consistent with punishments. He got much of his discipline from coaches when he played sports and from those experiences, he learned to discipline himself. From middle school to high school, football became a major part of Piper's life and his coaches and teachers were surrogate fathers and big brothers. He had teachers at Berkeley High School, among them Hodari Davis, Quamé Patton, and Antwi Akom, who are all strong leaders in the Bay Area community. Piper received advice from people who cared about him being the best that he could be. Coach Roy Wittke passionately insisted, "Finish!" Coach Thomas Coleman demanded his players have a "sense of urgency." Piper attributes that care to his success.

## *Jinho Ferreira: If enough cared about the violence in Oakland, it would be stopped*

*By Jinho Ferreira, guest commentary © 2013 Bay Area News Group*
*POSTED: 05/18/2013 08:00:00 AM PDT*

*The first time I held a gun I was 11. It was heavy and silver, a revolver. My older cousin was a pretty Black girl in Oakland coming of age during the crack epidemic. This means all of her boyfriends were gangsters. She and Tommy had fallen asleep on the couch, his gun on the dresser. I made sure I put it back exactly the way I found it.*

*By age 12, I was bagging crack, but not because I was a drug dealer. My best friend and I had tried out for a Pop Warner football team; he didn't make it. Two weeks later, he was dealing. I helped him bag it while playing video games. By 9th grade he had a baby; since then, he has been shot on six separate occasions.*

*When I was 13, I was looking up to the most notorious drug dealers in West Oakland. Most were between 17 and 25 years old, the youngest 14. I was what you would call a "little homie." I was by no means a gangster, but I loved feeling like one.*

*One day, the 14-year-old's mother discovered he was selling crack. I still remember the emptiness I felt when she chastised him for giving his money to "these little hoes" instead of giving it to her. My mother would have killed me. His mother died of AIDS a couple years later. He's now serving 36 years in prison.*

*My mother had three children, worked all day and was tired all night. In the 'hood, some parents collect a check from the government and are never home, other parents work two jobs and are never home. Either way, the streets have a way of raising us all. No matter how tired, my mother had a way of sensing when I was drifting too far. One day she demanded I be home for dinner. Later that night I received a call from one of my mentors. Somebody got killed. The older homies wouldn't be around for a while. Thanks, Mom.*

*After the entire older crew was convicted of murder, I remember all of us "little homies" deciding whether we would inherit the block or walk away. I walked away.*

*Not because I'm smarter, or more humane than the others. I was able to walk away because enough people cared enough to put in enough time, resources, and energy to make me decide to walk away.*

*In other words, the sum of all of the above tragedies that occurred in my life before reaching high school was not greater than the positive impact of people who demanded greatness from me. They shared their light and it inspired me to live.*

*There is a poison in the 'hood. It is a deadly concoction that encourages dehumanization. However, it would not exist if many of the most powerful people weren't asking themselves questions like, "Does it make more economic sense to do nothing?*

*What is an acceptable murder rate? Not ethically acceptable, but acceptable to the extent that it does not drive away corporate investors. How many teenage prostitutes are too many? To what degree does the number of arrests for prostitution or reported robberies in a given area drive down property value? Does it make more economic sense to alleviate prostitution in area A or B? Does it make more economic sense to do nothing?"*

*The truth about violence in Oakland is, if enough cared enough to put in enough time, resources and energy, it wouldn't exist.*

Growing up in West Oakland during the 1980s and 1990s, Piper lost many friends who were involved in underground economies to gun violence. Because of the death rates of young black males, it is said to be a gift to make it to age 25. There is also the idea that going to college will provide better quality of life outcomes.  Yet, some of his brothers and friends crossed the threshold, reached 25, went to college, and still met their fates searching for freedom. His brother Ricardo Lavender had attended San José State and wanted to become a fire fighter. He lost his life in a motorcycle accident at age 27. His brother-in-law Elijah

Warren was a special operations sergeant for the army who was fluent in Arabic. He was 26 and a senior at UC Berkeley majoring in political Science when he committed suicide. Piper's high school friend Jihad Akbar was a government and politics graduate from UC Berkeley. Tripping out on speed, he jumped over a counter at a restaurant, grabbed some knives, and in a suicidal act he charged police officers. He was 28 when the police killed him. The newspaper article said he was a homeless man shouting racial and homophobic slurs. Those who weren't familiar with Jihad's confrontational and sarcastic personality would have been confused to find out that he was a homosexual man and a social justice activist. Another friend since the 7th grade, Marcus Holland, was a graduate of Morris Brown and had a baby on the way. He died in a car accident with his cousin Anthony, who was also Piper's friend. They were drunk and high. Eddie Campbell, a probation officer for Alameda County, got his Master's in Public Administration and was in Puerto Rico for his future brother-in-law's bachelor party. An altercation erupted and someone shot Eddie in the head and the chest.

Another incident intimately impacted Piper's views on law enforcement. Anthony "Jimmy" Quintero was a childhood friend. A husband and a father, he worked security for an armored vehicle. Jimmy's work partner set him up and Jimmy was murdered in an armored truck robbery. Piper and his mom accompanied Jimmy's family to the court trial. Piper entered the courtroom and sat with the victim's family. He and his mother were the only black people seated amongst Jimmy's Mexican family. The suspect's family's side was all black. Piper remembered this being the first time in his entire life when he wanted a black person to go to jail.

His friends were men who had a similar understanding of what it was like to grow up in Oakland at the same time Piper did.  They were all people who were in his corner. Losing so many friends in his peer group put pressure on him to make his life meaningful. Through all of the pain and loss, his art and his problem-solving actions have always been his therapy.

When I met Piper, he was a juvenile hall counselor, a commercial writer at Carol H. Williams Advertising, and Dean's list student at San Francisco State University working to complete his Bachelor's degree in Black Studies. His band Flipsyde was also on the brink of signing with Interscope, which is distributed by Universal Records, the biggest label in the entertainment business.

Piper rented studio time at various studios and one of them, Soundwave in West Oakland, had a bar where artists from different genres would congregate. It was there that he met David López, a guitarist from Richmond, California. They made the type of music that could only come from the Bay Area: political hip-hop and Latin rock fusion. Though other artists have come and gone, at its core, Flipsyde is Piper and Dave.

Piper is the rapper, the writer, and the mind behind Flipsyde. He not only wrote the majority of the lyrics, Piper has keen business sense and he knows how to deal with people in the entertainment industry. His lyrics to "U.S. History" were published in San Francisco State University's Journal of Black Studies in 2004. He wrote and performed a solo song that dealt with a male perspective on abortion called "Happy Birthday." The song does not claim pro-life or pro-choice but in what can be considered Piper's signature style, it explores different perspectives on the issue. "Happy Birthday" topped the charts in several countries in Europe and Asia. Though he was presented with the idea of releasing it as a solo endeavor, he put the band on his back and added it to the *We the People* album instead. He truly believed in the band's potential to reach the world. He saw that a multi-racial, blue-collar band and their message of coming together were distinctive and particularly appreciated internationally.

> "Losing so many friends in his peer group put pressure on him to make his life meaningful."

If Piper is the brain, Dave López is the heart of Flipsyde. Dave is the laid back lead guitarist, who lives and breathes music. Dave's Chilean roots are infused in his guitar riffs, the wine he drinks, the way he warms up a room, and the way he cracks jokes and tells stories. One of the ironies in Dave's career as a musician is that he and the guitarist from Green Day both failed a guitar class from Contra Costa College. It was poetic justice that Dave got a chance to confront his former instructor when he saw him on the flight to Brazil just after Flipsyde got signed. Dave is the one who saves all of the Flipsyde music, articles, and paraphernalia. He is also the one who tries to preserve relationships. Piper and Dave would spend hours communicating with their fans on Facebook. The two represented the Bay Area through and through.

Though Piper and Dave are extremely talented the United States did not know how to handle a band like Flipsyde. Once they were signed in 2004, radio stations hardly played Flipsyde's music because of an American airwave dilemma. Hip-hop stations said Flipsyde had too many guitar solos. Rock stations said Flipsyde had too much rap. Alternative stations, such as the Bay Area's 105.3, took a chance on Flipsyde and found that their single "Someday" reached the Top 5. When Flipsyde went on tour, they discovered that international stations had fewer limitations. Their album *We the People* went gold in India. In fact, the Indian Universal division made a special edition of their album that featured Flipsyde music in Bhangra versions. The band was invited to perform several times in Japan, and they toured most countries in Europe playing at festivals to some audiences of more than 100,000 people with some of the biggest names of the time. In total, Flipsyde sold over one million singles and albums combined. Flipsyde received radio and MTV video play abroad as their music did not have to fit into a box.

The 2006 Winter Olympics proved to be an arena where Flipsyde music would find respect at home. "U.S. History," a song Piper wrote to teach youth in juvenile hall about war, and Flipsyde's hit song "Someday," were selected as theme songs. They continued to enjoy placements in the 2008 Summer Olympics, the films *Never Back Down* and *She's the Man*, the television show *Heroes*, several video games, and the Ultimate Fighting Championships commercials. After the second album came out in 2009, Flipsyde was released from the record label.

Never one to sit idly, Piper put his creative genius into other projects along with his music. He nurtured his love of languages by learning to read and write Arabic and Spanish. Piper wrote a screenplay called *Walter's Boys*, an action-packed thriller that won the Tribeca Film Festival that same year. He earned his black belt in Blossom Fist-style kung fu from Grandmaster Sifu Bill Owens. Piper was reading incessantly and developed an independent educational album.

Since Piper and I have been a couple, he has supported my teaching efforts by volunteering to work with the youth at my schools. My take as an educator was that the youth had to be educated, not just taught how to read but that they needed to have knowledge of the criminal justice system and how their choices could impact their lives. Teaching in the Bay Area, as in most urban areas, has provided its own set of challenges. My colleagues and I lost students to gun violence, prostitution, and jail. After the first shooting involving our students took place, our school mental health therapist found that 99% of our students displayed symptoms of post-traumatic stress disorder (PTSD).  This meant that students and teachers were all trying to function in a traumatized climate of pain, anger, loss, and struggle.

"After the first shooting involving our students took place, our school mental health therapist found that 99% of our students displayed symptoms of post-traumatic stress disorder."

I called on my husband, and he brought in his brothers and friends, some of whom are the deceased peers who were previously mentioned, to teach my students self-defense tactics and literacy. My predominately black male students would usually come from a black female-run home to a white female-run school to the streets where the authorities were typically white and male. Similar to the way that Piper had role models who cared about him, I saw first-hand how a strong force of black men could positively affect our youth.

# THREE

# BLACK AND BLUE

On January 1, 2009, BART (Bay Area Rapid Transit) police officer Johannes Mehserle shot Oscar Grant, an unarmed man. Mehserle claimed he mistook his gun for his Taser. Reminiscent of the Rodney King beating, several people caught the police encounter on videotape, but Oscar Grant was killed. Staying true to the formula: the cop was white, the victim was black, and the black community was outraged.

Piper and I went to the protests. Journalist Davey D interviewed Piper amongst other Bay Area rappers. When the question about how to stop unnecessary violence against black people by the police came up, Piper responded that he wanted to be policed by people who knew him, knew the community, and cared about the community. If no one in law enforcement thought like us how could we expect officers to act like we wanted them to act?

[View the video clip at: https://www.youtube.com/watch?v=Wu-NSij9wDk.]

My husband and I talked incessantly about how we could affect real change. It was like a game of logic—if racist, trigger-happy, dirty cops exist in America, and we could fire all of them, who would replace them? Piper remembers looking around at all of the protesters and thinking that he had never considered replacing them, nor did he believe anyone at the protest would replace them. If people who loved justice enough to protest brutality were not willing to become police officers, then it was highly probable the change we were searching for would not occur. Ultimately, this would mean all of our protesting was in vain.

Piper does not like doing anything in vain.  He is also extremely impatient.  Wanting to see true change happen right now, along with his background of being a martial artist and a communicator, he started exploring the notion of becoming a police officer.

The idea of my husband, an internationally known hip-hop artist being a cop was still too far-fetched. When we talked about him going into law enforcement, I had a tremendous fear regarding him risking his life. Along with that fear, was a sinking feeling that my husband would be joining what I, and many of the people in our community, believed was a white, racist fraternity. Extremely protective of my husband, I felt that Piper would be bearing the burden of representing our community by himself. Knowing how talented and intelligent my husband is, I did not want him to be in a place where he would be a subordinate to an ideology that he did not believe in.

People see the injustice in education and decide to become teachers. However, it seemed rare that a critique of law enforcement was countered with the revolutionary act of becoming a cop. During the days of the Jim Crow South, black people had their own schools, teachers, and principals. Some of the greatest black thinkers were nurtured, cultivated, and produced by black educators in segregated one-room schoolhouses. The focus of desegregation was on the students and not the power structure of the schools. This meant thousands of black teachers and black principals lost their jobs and their collective knowledge and expertise was devalued and ignored. White teachers and white principals without knowledge of black history and culture were then responsible for educating and disciplining black students.

> "...it seemed rare that a critique of law enforcement was countered with the revolutionary act of becoming a cop."

Recognizing racial injustice, my first teaching job was at a school in the Central Valley where a racist gang called the Peckerwoods burned an effigy of a black girl who was running for student body president. It was an agricultural community with a mix of suburban and rural white families, the children of Latino immigrants, and a sprinkling of black families. I chose to teach at this particular school because I wanted to combat racism and negative stereotypes. I held myself to standards of excellence as I taught French and Spanish and took on extra-curricular activities that particularly served the black students and students of color. As the first black teacher in the school's history, I received an anonymous death threat. I had seen the Ku Klux Klan ride horses on Fresno State University's campus.  I had gotten into debates with people who proudly displayed the confederate flag while selling fruit on the side of the road.  Two white men in a truck tailed my car on the freeway and drove me off of the road.  I attended a district-wide diversity training with a majority of white teachers who had no idea why we were having the training because their lives were not affected negatively by racism.

Because of my profound realization that educators needed to have an understanding of black children to teach them, I began to understand how important it was for police officers to understand the community that they policed.  I did not think anyone was having the critical conversations about the justice system that we were having at home. Piper began to research the possibilities of joining a police academy.

The application process can be six to eight months long entailing a grueling series of interviews; physical, psychological, and intellectual tests; and a stringent background check complete with a lie detector test. There is a 90-95% failure rate among applicants. If hired, applicants become "affiliates" and are paid to complete a police academy. Of those hired, about 20% fail the academy. The other option is to register as a "non-affiliate" for an academy and pay $5000. The "non-affiliate" position is precarious. Failing means time, energy, and money are lost. Success does not guarantee employment; it only means entering a pool with others who have completed the academy.

Piper joined the Alameda County Sheriff's Office (ACSO) Academy in Dublin, one of the most widely respected academies in the nation, as a non-affiliate. I thought the academy was fine because we believed that the knowledge that we gained became our family's knowledge. I thought it would be good for Piper to get the training that police officers get but a part of me did not expect him to be hired. I knew that he had been arrested before. I knew that anyone who searched could find a YouTube video of him rapping with his shirt off in front of large marijuana plants on the Snoop Dogg tour. I knew that a large portion of Flipsyde's material was extremely political. I was sure law enforcement agencies would shy away from hiring Piper. We talked to our family and friends and everyone thought we were crazy but no one was able to present a good enough argument for Piper not to do it. The brothers and friends that he could have imagined accompanying him on this journey and going through the academy with him had died. He was representing them; he was representing us, all by himself.

He went into a culture expecting the worst but found that some of the most unsuspecting people had his back. This included some instructors as well as academy members. Monday through Friday all day for seven months, he ran miles, fought, drove, shot, studied the law, and studied policy. He met people who were so set on becoming police officers that they had sometimes gone through an academy in the past, failed, and tried again. Piper humbly took the academy on with everything he had, never mentioning that he was a hip-hop artist who had toured internationally. The videos would circulate later—after all, this was the police.

People failed out weekly generally due to issues with physical performance, academic showing, or character deficiencies. Piper went so hard physically that he tore his calf muscle halfway through but finished limping to second overall. He studied so rigorously that our boys looked to him as an example of how to approach their own homework. Piper showed so much heart that his class elected him to deliver the commencement speech. In his memorized speech, he described the courage and bravery of those around him and what it meant to be a warrior. Piper reminded his classmates that the responsibility to serve and protect a community is paramount. He presented the notion of an ideal world where communities chose who policed them. The sheriff announced that it was the best commencement speech that anyone had ever given. I knew that Piper more than proved himself in the academy. There was something beautiful about seeing how my husband's effort paid off after seeing him put his work tirelessly into Flipsyde just to have it fall apart. Flipsyde was a collective of individuals in an industry that he had no control over, but in the field of public safety, Piper's physical and mental acumen earned him the respect he deserved.

I began to look at Piper being a public safety officer from a different angle. A true revolutionary puts his life on the line to change the system. Though some define revolutionary acts as writing or talking about change, Piper took action.  Though he does not consider himself a revolutionary that is how I saw my husband. Piper would be carrying a gun, risking his life, and doing the work that we had been allowing a force of predominately white men from the outside to do. Yet, he would be performing these acts guided by a love for his community.  He would be stepping up as a man who had made his share of mistakes and could mentor young black men. He would be able to discern his gun from his Taser. He would not be working in a community of people that he feared. Piper becoming a cop would challenge the black community's views on what a cop could be.

Shortly after graduation, ACSO informed Piper that he had earned the position of deputy sheriff. ACSO deputies work in many areas such as the courts, the Peralta colleges, the ports, the bus routes, the airport, the streets, and the jails. When deputies are hired, their first placement is in the jails. Here I was, just getting accustomed to the idea that my husband would be a law enforcement officer and his first assignment would be as a jail guard.

This was difficult for me to accept because of my philosophical opposition to the prison industrial complex. The United States locks more of its population up than any other country in the world. The bloated California prison budget has nearly bankrupted the state. Stringent policies have filled prisons with people who have committed non-violent crimes. Though crime reports state that crime is on the decline, prisons are overcrowded. Incarceration has become a huge industry from which many families are destroyed and many entities profit. Prison populations allow small towns to claim higher populations and receive more government services. Pharmaceutical companies, phone companies, food companies, vending machine companies, and many other corporations benefit. Bail bond companies benefit. Health care professionals benefit. Mental health care providers benefit. Prison teachers and clergy members benefit. The foster care system benefits. Attorneys benefit. Now, Piper and I would also benefit. I felt conflicted but I firmly believed in my husband. I took solace in the fact that he was safer working in the jails than on the streets and saw it as a steppingstone. What was initially a source of frustration for both of us, later enlightened and renewed in us a sense of purpose because of our connection to a broken system.

ACSO deputies typically work twelve-hour shifts, four days on and three days off, then three days on and four days off. When cops first start out, they get the least desirable positions like Piper's 5:00PM-5:00AM shift, every other Wednesday and every Thursday to Sunday. Our children and I would try our best to go through our morning rituals in silence, trying not to wake him. An hour to work and an hour back, Piper's commute to and from work added two hours to an already impacted day. When Piper got off of work he would call me in the morning and we would talk, making sure he made it home without falling asleep. The stories he brought home would challenge my belief that everyone could be rehabilitated. When we had been burglarized and my computer with the first iteration of my dissertation was stolen, I still believed that more employment and more social programs would solve the problem of crime entirely.

Piper told me about people who actually deserved to be in jail. These were not political prisoners or people who had been wrongly convicted. He described a man who knowingly had HIV but continued to sodomize children. Piper told me about youngsters who laughed about shooting innocent bystanders and pimping young girls while they played cards. Some may have suffered from PTSD, but their attacks on others necessitated confinement, separation from the community.

There were other stories Piper told that revolved around the basic core of human survival—food. He talked about grown men with mental health issues who could be calmed down from a murderous rage with chocolate chip cookies. He told me about former "ballers," or leaders, on the street, unable to conceive of working for minimum wage, who were happy to mop floors for an extra bag lunch because this was the equivalent of being a "baller" in jail.

Piper explained that jails were segregated by crimes and by race. There was minimum, medium, and maximum security along with administrative isolation. He said that some people were brought in on charges for minor offenses but both inmates and deputies alike knew they were murderers that just hadn't been caught yet. Inmates self-segregated just as most high school students did, but in jail it was to an extreme degree. Just eating lunch with someone from a different race could get an inmate severely beaten or slashed by members of his own race.

He would tell me when he came across one of my former students or a youth from juvenile hall that he used to counsel. They were literally a captive audience for any knowledge or advice he could provide to them. He talked about the brilliance of the inmates who could freestyle rap and make a complex beat at the same time. However, it seemed that the demeaning aspects of jail were always left out of the verses. He saw inmates employ resourcefulness by assembling a shank using a Styrofoam plate, toilet tissue, and toilet water. While another created a fire using an outlet, pencil lead, and toilet tissue before passing the fire underneath a cell door. My husband opened up the cell door to find an inmate smoking a joint. Piper, the same artist who spoke out for the oppressed on a major record label, began to question when anyone complained about the lack of opportunities because he saw men in jail create something out of nothing on a daily basis.

Looking at the numerous black bodies locked up, my husband could not help but think about slavery. The painful difference was that in the jail, many of the inmates were there more so because they had committed crimes against people who looked like them than because they were black. A large number of them had raped, killed, robbed, enslaved through drugs, or in some way violated other black people.

Three little boys under age six, Carlos Nava, Hiram Lawrence, and Gabriel Martínez, Jr. were killed and Piper did not see the same uproar from the community that took place when a police officer killed Oscar Grant. Innocent babies' lives were stolen because young men did not care about who received a bullet. Piper started to ask questions like, "How can we expect anyone to value black life when it appears as if black people don't even value their own?" This angst led to his song "Act Like A Cop Did It" where he speaks to the community about having the same anger about gun violence perpetrated by members of the community as when it comes from the hands of police officers.

Piper could sense that many other deputies were uneasy around him. They all knew his background. This could be a good thing because if there were racist jokes told or unnecessary uses of force they would never occur around my husband.

While Piper seems to be well-respected by some of the men and women that he works with, in many ways, I know that he must watch his back at all times. On one hand, I do not want him to get stabbed in the back by other cops who are jealous of his creativity and his connections to the community. If law enforcement officers cannot accept that my husband is a cop, they must be in policing for the wrong reasons. On the other hand, I do not want him to be stabbed in the back by people from the community who are confused about his intentions. If the black community doesn't want somebody like Piper to be the police, they don't want anyone to be the police; which is an unrealistic solution to real problems.

We had purchased our home in West Oakland as a way of taking action in our community before Piper became a cop. Piper's mom lived three streets up from us and his uncle lived one street down from us. We built relationships with our neighbors. We attended neighborhood meetings. We picked up after people who disposed of their litter in our yard. We hired ex-convicts to do our landscaping. Piper made sure that people did not congregate on the corner in front of our house. I asked the neighborhood children how they were doing in school. We had seen the drug-dealing move from our block to the next one over. A few of my students lived down the street from us. They did Cutco demonstrations in our living room. They brought their babies over. We were the couple who lived in and served our community or, "our 'hood."

However, raising children in the 'hood is difficult. We taught our children not to use drugs but drug dealers posted on several corners. We taught our boys to respect women, but down the street people pimped girls. Some youngsters did not go to school, but we taught our boys to strive for academic excellence. At ten, our oldest son asked why grown men glared at him like they wanted him to put his head down. He was referring to the hard facial expression, the "mean mug" that black men direct toward other black men. Our youngest son asked why the scantily clad girl at the bus stop did not have a jacket on.

On separate occasions, one of our family's cars and our front gate were totaled because intoxicated youth were driving down the wrong side of the street. We had encountered a stray bullet that went through four walls of our home and witnessed a drive-by shooting that happened a block away.

We were burglarized. Our computers and my husband's gun were stolen. Every night when I kiss my children good night I tell them, "You're loved. You're warm. You're far away from harm." After the burglary, my children felt like I was a fraud. I had to explain to them that the thieves did not want to hurt us because they broke in when we were not home and that they must not have received the same kind of love that my children received. I cried myself to sleep. I was sure that there was someone who knew who did it but was reluctant to snitch.

Our lives were vulnerable and filled with anxiety but after Piper became a full-fledged cop, being in West Oakland got harder. When an officer commits to work for public safety, his or her whole family is committed too. As a family, we came to the realization that dinner together would be inconsistent. Dad would not make it to the boys' games, performances, or parent-teacher conferences. There are no holidays off, so sometimes we took family trips and often attended social gatherings without him. Conversations with Piper would be succinct, only sharing the very good or very bad news.

My husband was always concerned for our safety, but when he became a police officer, his anxiety grew even more pronounced. In part, because he received a police bulletin every week that let him know what crimes had been committed locally and who committed them. I remember attending a monthly read-in, which was a community gathering on a street corner in West Oakland not far from where baby Hiram Lawrence had been shot and killed. Elders and children accompanied by a DJ and drums congregated to inspire positivity and celebrate literacy by telling their favorite stories. I was pregnant with our daughter and brought our sons to the event. Like the other community members in attendance, I had faith that an event like this could suspend the drug dealing and gun violence that plagued our community. Piper disagreed. He came by and told us to leave immediately. He knew the area, knew what the gangsters in the area were about, and he believed that they would not hesitate to get lethal. He chided me for putting our family in danger. I was upset that my husband did not want me to participate in community events and I felt like an adolescent girl who was told she was not allowed to go to the dance. I thought Piper was overly paranoid. After the next month's read-in, a shooting took place. Gunshots flew leaving a mother and her child ducking behind a car to avoid being shot.

A strenuous work schedule meant that we were not together often and when I had to run the household by myself, Piper was constantly worried.  He was concerned about me bringing groceries in too late or our children falling asleep in the car and taking too long to get into the house. If I did not answer my phone he would think the worst had happened. Some of our neighbors were Piper's former inmates. He began to see people on our block in two categories: those who committed crimes and those who were victims of crimes.

Community members typically do not want to snitch because of an unspoken racial unity and if it leads to the arrest of gangsters they will live in fear of revenge. However, Piper is someone our community trusts and some neighbors wanted to tell him everything.  Since police officers are the ones actually confronting and arresting the gangsters, the possibility of revenge is always present.

On one occasion, our next-door neighbor flagged Piper down and told him that five young men had broken into another neighbor's home. When Piper approached them he saw that at least one of them had a gun. They had no idea that Piper was an off-duty cop and that he had a gun as well. Piper assessed the situation and knew that he might have to shoot. Luckily, he was able to talk them out of the burglary. The situation was tense because it could have ended in a violent way. He was seconds away from killing them, when he employed his verbal skills. Here he was one against five and it could have easily ramped up to an officer-involved shooting directly across the street from our home. He glanced up and saw that our boys were watching him the entire time from their bedroom window. Killing a person or being shot in front of our children was a situation that Piper wanted to avoid. Our days in West Oakland were numbered.

Piper started to meet other cops who had similar experiences. These were cops from Oakland who tried to serve the same communities that they lived in. This is what many people, who criticize law enforcement, including me, have promulgated. It sounds good. It looks good on paper. The reality is that it is already difficult for families who are not cop's families to live in the 'hood. For an officer's family, choosing to live in a neighborhood with a high crime rate is similar to placing a target on you and your family's back. It means living in an environment that is surrounded by people who participate in underground economies and despise law enforcement. In 2012, Piper was going into his second year as a public safety officer and the stagnant jail scene felt like a waste of his time. He longed to be on patrol where he felt like he would make more of an impact. My husband had long ago realized that the police were some of the most powerful people in the country. Cops can decide whether a person is going to live or die RIGHT NOW. If the report an officer writes is in line with the available facts and their agency's use of force policy then the Supreme Court of the United States of America will stand behind them. With that realization Piper decided, if there were going to be any officers riding around our community, with guns, the training to use them, and the authority to decide whether people in our community were going to live or die right now, it should be him.

In order to get to the streets, a deputy sheriff had to prove himself in the jails by taking on overtime shifts, volunteering for ride-alongs, committing to a tremendous amount of study, and showing initiative in various areas. With a regular police agency, upon graduation from an academy, officers enter a Field Training Officer (FTO) program where cops learn to police the streets, on the streets.  The program is rigorous and if they fail, they are fired and the department has wasted thousands of dollars training them. The process is different for deputy sheriffs.  Many deputy sheriffs will work their entire careers without ever being invited to participate in the FTO program.  Only 50% of the deputies who make it to the FTO program pass, and failing the street program means returning to the jails or the courts.  The elimination process for deputy sheriffs in the FTO program is more intense because if they fail the program, the sheriff's office does not lose a deputy, they are simply sent back to their previous workstation and another is called out to try his or her luck.

I could not support him in being eligible for an FTO program because I was immersed in working on my dissertation. I was on the verge of being timed out of my graduate program. I needed to finish my dissertation before May and I was pregnant with our third child, due in August. As I did my research on PTSD in urban classrooms, Piper was encountering a time of crisis for himself. We found ourselves trading off time with our children as if we were divorced. Every minute that he was off-duty, he was on-duty with our children. We both felt he was giving more to law enforcement than he was getting out of it and it seemed like the people he was risking his life to protect did not want *his* protection. During this extremely stressful time, he was boiling over with emotions and we could not find the time to sit down and talk anymore. With many of his brothers and confidantes deceased, he had very few people around him who could understand him. His art had always been his therapy yet he had little time for that. As a public safety officer who had chosen a profession to bring about change, Piper questioned whether or not art could create the type of change that was needed. I had often told him that he needed to create his own one-man show. Somewhere in the madness, in the chaos, he listened and produced the masterpiece known as *Cops and Robbers*.

# FOUR

# A GIFT

It took Piper four days to write the play. It was a purging of all of the emotions that had built up surrounding his decision to go into law enforcement, the negative reactions of some of the people he attempted to protect, and the concern for the family he loved. *Cops and Robbers* is evidence of Piper's profound knowledge of the various realms in his life.  This one-man play is a culmination of Piper's life experiences from growing up during the crack epidemic to becoming a police officer. He created 17 characters that represent law enforcement officers, the media, and the community. The community characters include young men who have been discarded by society and participate in underground economies. The community also includes a religious leader who echoes the voice of the critical race theorists who speak out against racism and shield some of the aforementioned young men. Another feature in the play is the African ancestor whose spirit is following the present-day generation in outrage demanding accountability.

After Piper had finished writing this one-man play, with twists and turns like a movie, he tracked down a drama instructor he had taken a class with as a teenager. Ami Zins is a personable, kind-hearted, and generous soul whose strong commitment to social justice underscores her diligent work in the film and theater industry. When Ami and her husband Lew Levinson, also a producer, director, and theater instructor, saw the play, they were in their words "blown away." Ami felt that she had just seen a real story unfold in front of her eyes. The characters felt so genuine and honest. She was impressed with how Piper knowledgeably, non-judgmentally embodied each persona's point of view. Never in all her years of theater had she seen an actor give such a complete portrayal of each character on a first read. Ami saw working on this play as a calling because of its power to transform the viewer. After keeping this project a secret for two months, Piper revealed the play to me, his family, and a select group of people. By this time, I had finished my dissertation and his play was the ultimate graduation gift. I was thankful that during a period of intense struggle, Piper managed to find an outlet for his frustration through his art.

*Cops and Robbers* showed that Piper could change the way that people in the audience envisioned law enforcement. The play is not a stand-up comedy routine that allows the audience to laugh off responsibility when they feel uncomfortable. This theatrical piece is confrontational, aggressive, and unapologetic. It shows Piper's belief in the intellectual capacity of his audience. Piper has encapsulated a necessary link between law enforcement, the media, and the black community—the ability to see a situation from different perspectives. Because of his unique position Piper was able to bring teachers students, law enforcement officers, street hustlers, journalists, paramedics, and politicians to his play.  The play conveys a message to a demographic that needs to hear the story and has the power to create change within law enforcement, the media, and the black community. Each character has a truth and by portraying such a plethora of characters, Piper lets everyone eavesdrop on the inner thoughts of someone who may hold a different opinion. Instead of launching into a reactionary debate, the audience is captivated, listening, and taking it all in. *Cops and Robbers* is more than a play; it is a gift to the community and a tool for change.

> "Each character has a truth and by portraying such a plethora of characters, Piper lets everyone eavesdrop on the inner thoughts of someone who may hold a different opinion."

# PHOTO GALLERY

From left to right:  Arion Salazar (founding member of Third Eye Blind), Dave López, Piper, and Reto Peter working on the Cops and Robbers EP at Reto's studio.  Dope!!!

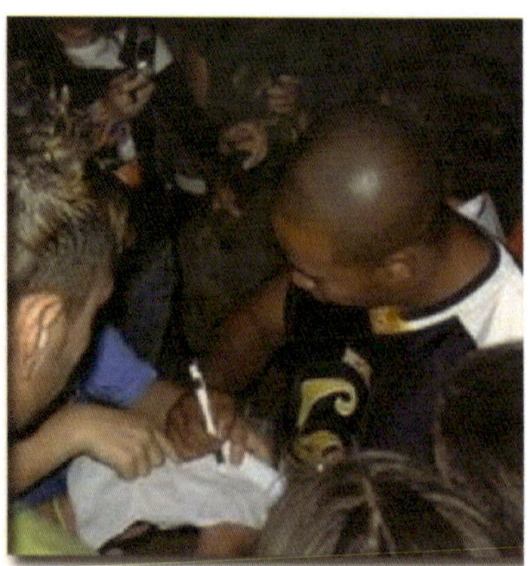

Piper signing autographs in India and representing UC Berkeley

Dave & Piper backstage on the Snoop Dogg/The Game/Flipsyde tour

Piper and Dave bring their music to the masses.

In 2007, there was a series of riots at San Quentin Prison.  The Lifers put together "A Day of Peace Festival" and asked Flipsyde to perform.

Dave López and Piper signing autographs in Italy

Flipsyde photo shoot on the roof of the old Soundwave Studios building at 21$^{st}$ & Union in West Oakland

Flipsyde Fan Art

Inmate Art:  A yo-yo made by inmates, using unknown materials

Inmate Art:  They mixed water, ashes, and pencil lead.

Inmate Art:  This rope made from toilet tissue is actually strong enough to strangle someone.

Inmate Art:  Purse made in Santa Rita Jail out of Top Ramen packets.  Some inmates don't have anyone to put money on their books so they make and sell purses like these to other inmates.

Inmate Art:  Dragon made out of candy

Inmate Art:  Rose made of candy

Inmate Art:  A shank.  Some inmates are less artistic than others and just stick to making weapons.

Inmate Art:  Spiderman figure made from sock and shirt thread

Inmate Art:  Dice made from candy

Our former home in West Oakland, where both good and bad memories were made

Our old neighborhood was informally called "Ghost Town."  This name is reminiscent of the Wild West and many young Black lives that have been taken in this area.

Piper, according to Dawn, is the most hardworking man in the world.  When he is not in uniform, on stage, or at home, he is typically in the studio.

Piper, in "Marc Dub" character

Beloved directors, Ami Zins and Lew Levinson

# MAIN CHARACTER BACKSTORIES


# THE AFRICAN ANCESTOR

**AFRICAN ANCESTOR**

In the village from which I descend, a boy could not become a man just because he had his birthday.

*It was customary for pre-colonial African civilizations to require a significant rite of passage as a prerequisite to enter adulthood. In fact, some cultures banished those boys and girls deemed too weak or unsuited to pass into adulthood. The boys that failed were at the very least not allowed to marry, at most, exiled from their village. When these ancient practices are compared to contemporary*

*African American and American mainstream culture, the irony lies in the fact that today boys and girls who shirk or postpone the responsibilities of adulthood are often publicly worshipped and idolized. American popular culture is overrun with young, and sometimes not so young, superstars that preach the gospel of irresponsibility.*

*While the desire for eternal youth is not a new phenomenon, when its contemporary Western form is set against Ancient African traditional systems the paradox is clear. The image of the irresponsible, shortsighted, short-tempered, oversexed, seeker of instant gratification boy is undoubtedly preferred to the prudent, consistent, hardworking and responsible man. Record labels and film studios spend billions of dollars annually in an effort to maintain this paradigm. He who would have been unfit for marriage (procreation) in pre-colonial Africa, is now widely considered to be an alpha male and an object of desire by many women.*

## AFRICAN ANCESTOR

In the village from which I descend, a boy could not become a man without weapon in hand and a will to defend the past, present, and the future. He would all too willingly lay down his life to serve as a bridge for the children to cross, continuing the eternal march of a people who have always been and will always be. He could not fathom the selling of an adolescent girl's body in the street. Surely that would mean banishment from the village! He would be confused by gunshots over shoes, and the village griots rapping about it; justifying it. He would not know how to, "Keep it real." He was taught to reach for excellence!

*Here the African ancestor describes the values of the warrior class of many African civilizations: Ghana, Mali, Songhai, Dahomey, Dogon, Zulu, Nubia, Kemet, etc. Note that he refers to the young warrior defending the past, present and future. This can mean many things; children, adults, and elderly; history of a people, current political state/ambitions of a people, and future projections for a people. It has individual meaning as well; remembering who you were, knowing who you are, striving toward your own personal transformation.*

*What is paramount here is the African ancestor describes the warrior class as a bridge for the "children" to cross from the "past" into the "future." The warrior class (young adults) are the conduits through which the wisdom and mastery of the elders is able to mold the malleable minds and spirits of the highly impressionable youth. Following this truth, the warrior class serves as the psychological protectors of a culture, the physical protectors of a people, and the driving force of progress.*

*When viewing the warrior class through this lens, the African ancestor is unable to conceive of one of its members "selling an adolescent girl's body in the streets." The African ancestor cannot fathom a warrior preying on an adolescent girl that he has previously taken an oath to die for if necessary.*

*Though he mentions the "greatest crime of the millennium," he does not fully understand how centuries of slavery have transformed the value system and the reality of the sons and daughters of Africans in America. The African ancestor sizes up the situation and springs into action:*

## AFRICAN ANCESTOR

And as he moves to banish the wicked from the village, he is surprised when the village turns to kill him. They are addicted to the rum and the chains and the guns, even the adolescent prostitutes are against him. In the village from which I descend, honor was buried deeply within the breasts of men, like a treasure. And if you cannot dig that, then you will never find it.

*The African ancestor explains what happens when modern day warriors attempt to banish the wicked (all those that act in opposition to the original value system) from the village. They find that the predators, and surprisingly their prey, are united in solidarity against them. They have all succumbed to a newer value system, which ironically happens to be the same system that allowed for the destruction of their original system and subsequently left them in physical slavery.*

*The African ancestor warns, "And if you cannot dig that, then you will never find it." This is a nod to the power of history as an antidote. If the modern village has no knowledge of what it once was, or how it came to be, then it will remain enslaved forever.*

# EMMA INSTI'GATOR

**EMMA**

We're standing here outside of the old Oakland auto plant. What was once a source of employment for many Oakland residents is now a crime scene.

*At the time I wrote this play, I had not heard of any old auto plants in Oakland California. As far as the story is concerned, the existence of an actual, physical auto plant in Oakland is irrelevant. My focus was to capture the absence of a one-time powerful blue-collar industry that once served as an economic backbone of black communities across country, and have it serve as the capsule for this modern day tragedy.*

*In Pulitzer Prize-winning journalist Eugene Robinson's book* Disintegration, *he writes, "The Big Three automakers were the economic lifeblood of the region and an abundant source of steady, good-paying jobs for African Americans—an escalator, in effect, that led directly to the middle class." Oba T'Shaka lists the relocating of several blue-collar industries to the suburbs, overseas, or the prison system, as one of the many "highly sophisticated external forces that hit the black community post-1968."*

*The absence of a blue-collar industry employing large sectors of the black community is a fact. In this play, the only event that everyone can agree on is what happens inside the old auto plant. Everything else is spin, opinion, or a truth that at best has only an indirect relationship with the central conflict of this play.*

### EMMA

Witnesses say that an Oakland police officer shot a man across the street from this plant, the man then returned fire, wounding the officer, and managed to escape into the plant. Witnesses then say that the officer gave chase, and neither the man nor the officer have emerged from the plant since. A small crowd is beginning to form outside, and they are now being pushed back by a swath of police officers. There are ambulances, fire trucks, officers from various agencies on scene and at this time I am being told that we have no further information. Please stay tuned for developments in this amazing, I mean crucial story. This is Emma Insti'gator, with I-Start-It News.

*Although "Emma Insti'gator" is new to the job, she is clear on what is expected from her: ratings. In my Terrorism and Covert Politics class, I learned that in order for the press to be successful it must "Begin with blood and guts, follow with controversy, and end with a puppy."*

*As I later began studying screenwriting, I noticed the similarities between the nightly news and Hollywood blockbusters. Most great stories are told in three acts: the hook, the controversy, and the resolution. Like the puppy, the resolution is supposed to leave the audience with a warm and fuzzy feeling of completeness and optimism. Act 2, the controversy, is the longest of the three. The longer you can introduce new twists and continue to maintain the viewer's attention, the more powerful the climax will be.*

*What is important to understand here is that Emma is not personally invested or attached to any of the "characters," she is simply the camp counselor telling stories by the campfire. If she is pretty, the children will stop to look at her. If the story is shocking they will pay attention. If it is simple enough for the dumbest of them to understand, they will love her. If it encompasses their greatest fears, desires, or even better, topics considered to be taboo, she will have their complete and undivided attention.*

*Emma knows that race is one of those topics Americans consider to be taboo. I often hear it said, so much it has become cliché, that Americans don't discuss race. In order for this statement to be true it would need to be altered to, "Americans don't discuss race, in the presence of those of a different race." Nearly everyone discusses race, has their personal opinions on the matter, and is conscious of how they express those opinions in public, especially when in the company of those of a different race. This is a contributing factor to why, as a whole, Americans' understanding of race is so infantile. Imagine a group of men standing around discussing women, in hopes that they might be able to understand them better. It's completely ridiculous to conceive they will ever get past an elementary understanding of the opposite sex without the input of women. When applied to race, this ignorance, reinforced by centuries of direct propaganda from the fields of Western psychology, education, and entertainment, have created the apathetic state necessary to execute what the African ancestor calls, "...the greatest crime of the millennium."*

*The black community is not monolithic. There is no one black Agenda. Yet, Emma Insti'gator knows how to unite black people (whether consciously or by instinct). She has a card to play: racism.*

*Eugene Robinson writes, "Ever wonder why black elected officials spend so much time talking about purely symbolic 'issues,' like an official apology for slavery? Or why they never miss the chance to denounce a racist outburst from a rehab-bound celebrity? It's because symbolism, history, and old-fashioned racism are about the only things they can be sure their African American constituents still have in common."*

*If Emma can make the conflict of Cops and Robbers about race, she will breathe life into a topic proven to unite the black community, while simultaneously calling to arms racism deniers who are 'tired of being blamed for the black community's failures.'*

*Emma makes true on her threat to the lieutenant of irresponsible journalism. In law enforcement, it is practice to separate witnesses to any event because of the human tendency to allow one person's recollection to affect another's. No two people will ever see the same thing, the same way. Emma knows this, but she needs information now. This is why it is also a practice of law enforcement to give the journalists something, before they create it themselves.*

*Emma ends this monologue by referring to the "man" in her opening statement, as the "victim", and in doing so, creates the largest political upheaval of her career thus far.*

*In a 2003 interview with UC Berkeley News, George Lakoff, the accomplished Linguistics professor and author, spoke on the importance of word selection. "Language always comes with what is called 'framing.' Every word is defined relative to a conceptual framework. If you have something like 'revolt,' that implies a population that is being ruled unfairly, or assumes it is being ruled unfairly, and that they are throwing off their rulers, which would be considered a good thing." Lakoff explains in his work that whether you argue for or against the revolt is less important than the subconscious framework attached to the word, which supports the "revolt" being "considered a good thing." Since most of our thinking is done subconsciously, one can begin to understand the importance of word selection and framing.*

*America is still fairly segregated as far as neighborhoods are considered. When speaking of the differences between the suburbs and inner city the contrast in cultures only deepens. Emma Insti'gator is the individual that everyone knows. She is the go between as far as communities, cultures, and geographically separated epicenters are considered. Without first hand knowledge of different communities and cultures we are all, to some degree, dependent on Emma Insti'gator to tell us the 'truth' about one another.*

# THE MINISTER

**MINISTER**

Now, what we have here, is a blatant example of
police terrorism at it's worst. You see, instead
of serving and protecting, they are murdering and
neglecting those that they should be most
obligated to serve and protect. They are shooting
first and leaving us to ask the questions later.
Holding open target practice in our streets,
amongst our children and elderly. But that is not
the worst of it. Oh no that is far from the worst
of it. You see, brothers and sisters,
unfortunately for us they have been committing
these atrocities in our communities for years.
But it has been a very long time since one of
these...officers of the law, has shot down one of
our brothers; one of our fathers, one of our
sons, our future leaders, simply for expressing a
symbol of our unity. I say simply for expressing
a symbol of our resistance! Oh my brothers and
sisters it has been a mighty long time since one
of these gangsters in blue has shot down one of

80

```
our brethren simply...for holding up a fist...of
Black Power.
```

*Before the rapper, with his swag and word play, there was the Baptist preacher and Muslim minister. The African griot's tradition of dramatic oral expression and verbal gymnastics is alive and well. It can be found anywhere from Cornel West's cadence, to Kendrick Lamar's "spittage," to Michael Eric Dyson's relentless delivery. It is powerfully magnetic and when applied to a beat, it becomes the most influential music in the world.*

*If I were to attempt to explain how I created the Minister in academic terms, I would say that I pulled from three sources: Pan-Africanism, Black Nationalism, and Malcolm X. Pan-Africanism encourages the solidarity of Africans worldwide. Black Nationalism advocates for a racial definition (or redefinition) of national identity, as opposed to multiculturalism. And Malcolm X whose hard-hitting logic and hypnotizing wordplay can stir the audience into a frenzy.*

*In actuality, the Minister was one of the easiest characters for me to write. I already knew everything he would say. He speaks from a position of black existence in a world dominated by Western values. The Minister does not waste time and energy on so-called isolated events. He sees black existence in a world dominated by Western values as a period lasting from the 1500s to the present day, roughly 500 years. Through his eyes, there are no isolated incidents.*

*The Minister remains focused on the elephant in the room, what he views as structural white supremacy. The Minister is not going to debate the species of insect clinging to the elephant's ass, or the insect's behavior before, during and after it affixed itself to the elephant's ass. The Minister demands the world acknowledge the existence of the elephant, because anything short of its acknowledgement is at best insignificant, at worst, deception.*

*This is why the Minister does not hesitate to speak before learning the many facts of the officer involved shooting. That would be like waiting to determine why the insect clung to a specific region of the elephant's ass. For the Minister, the officer involved shooting is just another example of structural racism in a long list of examples spanning 500 years.*

*The Minister's job is to keep community members focused on the "realities" of black existence in a world dominated by Western values. Sometimes the community loses focus and begins to celebrate small achievements that, when placed into a larger context, are nearly insignificant.*

*Some members of his community believe times have changed for the better. The Minister has a profound understanding of history and is aware of the ebbs and flows of black achievement in America. When the Minister is made aware that "the suspect was shot, by the Oakland Police Officer, while holding up a Black Power fist" he jumps at the opportunity to prove to his community that things haven't changed as much as they had previously thought.*

# ROB BOB

**ROB BOB**

Okay...so let me get this straight... this jack
hole, is running around, holding up a *Black* Power
fist, like some crazy, murderous, revolutionary
*Black* Panther from the sixties, who, by the way,
should all be dead or in jail by now. You know,
didn't we get rid of all you guys? Didn't the
*citizens* of the United States of America already
say we didn't want you? You gangsters that
claimed to be helping the *black* community but
were really just selling heroin and pimping
women. Many of them white women I might add. You
know, wasn't your leader, Huey *Pimp* Newton a drug
addict? Who was himself gunned down in the same
*black* community he claimed he was trying to save?

Yeah I guess they didn't want him either. You know, this is a joke. This is a total joke, and God bless that officer. God bless that officer who was shot by the suspect. Who I'm willing to bet anything is a parolee. Oh that's right he's a parolee. C'mon! He's a parolee. He's a parolee... that was released early by some liberal judge. Well that's the ninth circuit for ya. Oh, oh and I can hear 'em now. God help us, I can hear 'em now they're probably saying, *"Oh..Da brotha...oh, da brotha man, you see, oh da brotha man, ya see. Oh da brotha man he be, he be havin' his hands up. You see? Da brotha man he be havin' his hands up, and the PO-lice man, he be shootin' 'em, in the back."* Give me a break. Give me a freakin' break. You know, let me ask you a question; how is it that you can have your hands up when you're busy shooting at the police? Doesn't make sense does it? Doesn't make logical sense does it? Think people, think! Please! Use your noggin. Jesus criminy. Oh-ok. Ok, now just wait a second. Ok, now hold on just a minute... Okay, now I agree... he had one hand up, and that was the hand with the Black Power fist, but the other hand had a gun in it, and it was pointed at the police officer. Shooting at the officer! God bless that officer for his bravery, and may Lord Jesus Christ be with him, as he walks through the valley of death in that old auto plant. This is Rob Bob, taking your calls right now.


*In an attempt to understand Rob Bob, we must first understand how he was created. To be fair, there are several different types of Rob Bobs, each with their own backstories. There's the closed-minded East Coast Catholic Rob Bob, the Midwest factory working Rob Bob, so on and so forth. The following is one possibility of the near infinite number of backstories for the Rob Bob I created.*

*The contrast between the Minister and this Rob Bob is so great it is a mystery how they could have both been raised in the same country. At first glance their philosophies appear to be polar opposites, but a closer look will reveal they have many things in common.*

*Rob Bob, like the Minister, most likely comes from a long line of poor people struggling to make a living. Although his ancestors probably immigrated to the United States in hopes of making a better life for their children, it is also probable they were some of the thousands of European children and drunkards kidnapped and shipped off to North America as indentured servants. Either way, the chances are, they arrived at the mainland with little more than the clothes on their backs.*

*If they were indentured servants in the early 17th century Virginia, they ironically befriended, had relationships with, and worked alongside their African indentured servant counterparts. In fact, it wasn't until the latter part of the 1600s that the racism we have come to know in America was invented.*

*When the slave trade became recognized as big business by the governments of the most powerful sovereign nations of that time, the fields of education, psychology, philosophy, theology, medicine, entertainment, and the mainstream media set out to justify it. What followed was centuries of oppression that would not have been possible without the support and apathy of an extremely large demographic of Americans: poor whites.*

*The owners of America's wealth have always numbered in the few, not only dwarfed by the number of African slaves, but also severely outnumbered by the tens of millions of poor whites. Should the poor African and poor white ever unite, an actual redistribution of wealth may come into focus.*

*The centuries-long propaganda campaign against America's humanity has served several purposes. Initially, it was to isolate the African and maintain the system of slavery and at that time, it was generated by the wealthy and educated. As poor whites seethed with hatred over the thought of competing for jobs with a people they had already been conditioned to believe were inferior, the prototype for Rob Bob was born.*

*Still taking his cues from the wealthy, Rob Bob was able to communicate black inferiority to poor whites in a way his more well-off brothers could have only dreamed of. Financially speaking, Rob Bob did not directly benefit from slavery. Furthermore, Rob Bob's education level was such that he could not understand the many ways in which he indirectly benefitted from slavery. Rob Bob had no in-depth understanding of economics or history and because of this, he was unable to view the complex situation of race in America from a wider context.*

*Rob Bob may have been as poor as the African in America, and sometimes even less educated, but as long as he was white, he believed in his opportunity to realize the American dream. Rob Bob was reminded of his white superiority daily by concerted propaganda efforts emanating from the fields of education, psychology, philosophy, theology, medicine, entertainment, and the mainstream media. As far as Rob Bob was concerned, America was a white man's land, and it was his job to keep it that way.*

*Rob Bob's culture of white superiority rests on a conservative value system ironically similar to the Minister's in some aspects. Both believe in being accountable for one's self. Both believe prayer is useless without action. Both believe in marriage and tend to be against homosexuality. Both are extremely religious. Both believe their people are under attack, and they will defend them by any means necessary.*

*Rob Bob saw black advancement during Reconstruction as offensive in several ways. In the first sense, it is highly probable that Rob Bob would have fought in the Confederate Army during the Civil War, a war that killed over 600,000 Americans. If he did serve, it is almost certain that Rob Bob had seen his share of brutality and trauma. Rob Bob, like millions of other Americans, had lost friends and possibly family in the bloodiest war in America's history. If we had asked Rob Bob during that time period why the Civil War was fought, his response would've been something to the effect of, "Because the Yankees (white liberals and progressives), wanted to free the niggers."*

*The second reason why black advancement during Reconstruction was offensive to Rob Bob builds on the momentum of the first. Rob Bob, poor, unemployed and illiterate, feels he is passed over by a white man's government in a white man's land as it reaches out to its second-class citizens. The Freedman's Bureau, created by the Federal government to educate and employ recently freed Africans in America, began building several schools and colleges to service the recently freed slaves. The Bureau also gave newly freed slaves clothing, food, water, health care, jobs, and assisted them with tracking down family members. It distributed 15 million rations of food to African Americans (Goldhaber 1992) and set up a system where planters could borrow rations in order to feed freedmen they employed. Imagine as Rob Bob looked on from his dirt floor shack struggling to make ends meet. Rob Bob's commentary at the town bar in 1865 would not significantly differ from his talk radio show in 2013.*

*As tensions build between poor whites and poor blacks during Reconstruction, we begin to see blacks being elected to political office. Rob Bob, in his limited understanding of politics and history, completely ignores the exclusive group of white men that have occupied political office in America since its inception, and convinces himself the blacks are taking over.*

*In examining his logic, we find it is rooted in the reality of the very real separation of poor whites and wealthy whites. While holders of American political offices up to that point had largely been white men, very few of them had been poor. In other words, Rob Bob had already known and to some extent accepted the absence of his voice from the American political process.*

*While his near political impotence, illiteracy and poverty may have stung, Rob Bob could rest assured he was not the worst off in America. There was an entire race of people beneath him. Not because he had more money or knowledge, but simply because he was white. Rob Bob's whiteness allowed him the power to beat, rape or kill any black man or woman with impunity, unless of course they belonged to a wealthy white man. His whiteness held the possibility of the American dream enjoyed by wealthy whites, while simultaneously separating him from the bottom of the American socio-economic and political barrel.*

*The educational, economic and political advancement of poor blacks shattered the idea of security in his whiteness. Black advancement destroyed the only thing in this world that saved Rob Bob from being a "nigger."*

*Rob Bob attacked black advancement like his life depended on it. He created the Ku Klux Klan and spread the gospel of white supremacy. He armed himself and prepared for the imminent race war that he believed was sure to come any day. He warned that if the white man did not take swift and immediate action, this once great country would be lost to backwards thinkers, degenerates, and savages.*

*Rob Bob chanted for the ouster, by any means necessary, of black politicians and their white political allies, which culminated in the murders of several Republican politicians in the early 1870's, and most notably in the Mississippi election of 1875. With weapons purchased by wealthy whites, Rob Bob created enough havoc to force Governor Ames of Mississippi to request federal troops from President Grant. When Grant refused, Ames hopelessly fled the state and Mississippi was taken over by Rob Bob and his friends.*

*Rob Bob was fighting for his country and his dignity, but most of all his identity. He continues to do so today. While times have changed, Rob Bob's motives, beliefs and shortcomings have not. He continues to remain oblivious to the many ways in which he benefitted from slavery, which serves as partial motivation to attack government programs that benefit black people. He is still too ignorant to see that the identity of whiteness he so desperately fights to preserve, only has worth in relation to those that are oppressed by it. He continues to viciously attack independently thinking blacks that rise in the fields of politics and education, as well as their white, liberal allies. He continues to enjoy an agreement with wealthy whites in that they fund his efforts, and he in turn focuses the anger and frustrations of poor whites away from their true oppressors.*

# THE LIEUTENANT

**LIEUTENANT**

Sir! Indeed, sir! Absolutely, sir! I'm all over it, sir! Thank you, sir! Thank you, sir! Thank you, sir!

*(Lieutenant hangs up the phone)*

Goddamn it! Shit! Jesus Christ! Johnson, Taylor, get your asses in here! Close the goddamned door!

*(Attempt at whispering)*

You know, what in the hell is his problem? Going after a barricaded suspect, shot, alone, wounded? You know, this kid is so far outside of policy I can't reach him this time. I want everything on that goddamn suspect. He's gotta be on parole, probation, all his priors. He shot a fucking cop; he didn't just start his career today. Right? You

know, I wouldn't give a damn if all he did was
steal a bag of chips, I want it, I wanna spin it,
and I wanna get it to that bitch journalist
immediately she's killing us out there! What? No.
No, not now. No, goddamn it, no! Hey, listen
up... nobody let on the cop is black. Hey! Nobody
let on the cop is black. We're saving that, when
shit gets out of hand. I've played this game
before. Besides, we disclose now...we disclose
now... they spin it...he's an Uncle Tom
victimizing the community. They'll get it.
They'll get it. They'll pull his use of force
record...son of a bitch has done more shit than
anyone in the department. They get it, he'll be
done. No, we're gonna win this one...well what in
the hell you standing there lookin' at? We got a
man out there in a gun battle let's go goddamn
it. Get me something!

*This is one of my favorite scenes in the play because it highlights
the fact that in law enforcement shit rolls downhill. The lieutenant
gets his ass chewed off by one of the higher-ups, then he calls in
Johnson and Taylor to chew theirs off – classic.
The lieutenant's back is against the wall and he's constantly
thinking damage control. He's got an in-progress, officer-involved
shooting and the first thing that comes out of his mouth has to do
with policy. It's not his fault; all that stuff is hammered into his
head on a daily basis. It's just hilarious to see it play out in this
scene.*

*The Lieutenant takes the standard route in trying to dig up dirt on
the suspect. He clearly expects to find a history of violent priors,
but if not, anything will do. The goal is to reduce the people's
capacity to have empathy for the suspect. This will take some of the
fury out of the fire that is sure to come.*

*The withholding of information regarding the cop being black was
my own touch of fiction. I imagine if this were a real life event, the
police officer being black would be the first piece of information
released to the press.*

## MARC DUB

*Marc Dub is one of the most heinous characters in the play. Which is why it astounds me that he is also the most liked. No matter the race, socio-economic background or religious affiliation, audience members that have been polled, overwhelming point to Marc Dub as their favorite character. I have to admit, he's definitely entertaining.*

*I have known a few Marc Dubs personally, which is probably why he, along with the Minister, was one of the easiest characters for me to write. I always knew exactly what he would say and how he would say it.*

*Co-director of the play Ami Zins points to an inner conflict as the reason people gravitate toward Marc Dub. For example, some of his most memorable lines are, "Black Power, nigga!" and "They shot my nigga like he was just...a nigga. You feel me?"*

*Marc Dub describes how he and DeMariay McDaniels raped a 13-year-old girl and subsequently pimped her out to grown men. He then almost immediately states that if anyone ever did the same to one of his family members he would kill that person. We watch Marc Dub struggle to determine whether the shooting of DeMariay McDaniels was "Some hood shit, or some police shit." Whatever he ultimately decides, he already has a preconceived understanding of how to process the situation.*

## Marc Dub

And if it is some hood shit, then I ain't seen shit, I ain't heard shit; you feel me? Nigga, see no evil, hear no evil, speak no evil. You feel me? But now if it's police shit, then... nigga, somebody gotta say something. You feel me? 'Cause the police can't just be comin' through shootin' niggas like that, you feel me?

*This is hilarious because it reminds me of the rapper that makes 10 albums about selling drugs to, killing, and pimping black people. Then he proceeds to make a protest song when the police or any other non-black person kills a black person. From a business perspective, the rapper's risk-taking is apparent in that he's chosen to produce a product other than what his customers have consistently supported. His bravery should be applauded. But from a moral and ethical perspective it doesn't add up.*

*When I wrote Marc Dub, I wanted to capture the version of black man that America has chosen to place at the center of popular culture. Suburban kids in Nebraska love him because he is the king of a jungle in which they could never truly be allowed entrance. He tells them exciting stories about life, death, sex and power. Inner city black kids love him because he appears to be an extremely successful older version of them. His success is always viewed as attainable because it's almost always present on the radio, television, and in conversations with friends. I wanted to showcase the characteristics everyone loved about him while simultaneously revealing the nefarious side that comes with it.*

*Some rappers will tell you everything you need to know about going to the penitentiary—except for being stripped naked so some prison guard can look into their ass for contraband. They tend to not mention paying some of their commissary to whoever is running the pod to avoid ass whippings. They also leave out asking the shot caller for permission to use the phone or begging deputies and prison guards for an unpaid job mopping floors just so they can get out of their cells.*

*These are some of the examples of the lost verses we don't hear on the radio or on our favorite rappers' albums. This is the type of reality I had hoped to capture with Marc Dub's character.*

*I did not see Marc Dub as conflicted. He has a very clear interpretation of right and wrong. He just happens to be selfish, ignorant, and insane. Maybe his insanity is the real reason we like him so much. His insanity is actually entertaining. He is the culmination of all the negative events that have taken place in black America since the 1600's.*

# DEMARIAY MCDANIELS

**DEMARIAY MCDANIELS**

I ain't goin' back to jail. I grew up in jail. I was born with an umbilical chord wrapped around my wrist and fluid in my lungs so I couldn't say shit. They should've just let me die. What kind of sick muthafucka saves a life just to kill it a thousand times? My mama's mama was my mama and her daughter? Shit, she was just Tamika. Yeah, my father was *everybody* and *nobody*. Top Ramen and Malt-O-Meal, Now-or-Laters, I can't sit still. My mama say I'm special... and that's why... I'm in Special Education. The teacher taught me how to, how to get in line and shut up. Yeah, that's how I knew I didn't need school because I already knew how to get in the welfare line and shut up when the police is talkin' to me. I got hatred walkin' through me. Bubblin' to the surface, drippin' from my lips like vomited venom. This is the vernacular of a virgin who has never known love, but fucks the world everyday, in every way. And if you wanted your car stereo then you shoulda' kept the doors locked. And if you wanted your laptop then you shouldn't have brought it with you. And if you didn't want me to rape you, then you shouldn't have been home when I broke in. Or better yet, bitch, you shouldn't have let the world rape me. So fuck you!

*In the days preceding the writing of this play, I was reading a lot of Western philosophy and listening to the Last Poets. One night I sat down, picked up a pen and started writing. Minutes later, I had the above spoken word piece.*

I ain't goin' back to jail. I grew up in jail. I was born with an umbilical chord wrapped around my wrist and fluid in my lungs so I couldn't say shit.

*DeMariay McDaniels is the sum of all of the ghetto youth I have ever known. His monologue begins with an acknowledgement of his continuous incarceration. He touches on the complicated births and high mortality rates among infants of color in America's inner cities. He then combines that with the feeling of being voiceless.*

They should've just let me die. What kind of sick muthafucka saves a life just to kill it a thousand times?

*The most important word for me in the above sentence is "They". DeMariay views society as a whole, and himself as outside of it. Whether it's the doctors that saved him as a baby, the teachers that couldn't get through to him, or police officers locking him up — "They" are all the enemy.*

My mama's mama was my mama and her daughter? Shit, she was just Tamika. Yeah, my father was *everybody* and *nobody*.

*If you work with inner city youth in any capacity you are familiar with some children referring to their grandmother as "mama", and to their mother by first name. The phrase regarding his father*

*refers to many men sleeping with his mother, but none assuming
the responsibility of being a father.*

Top Ramen and Malt-O-Meal, Now-or-Laters, I can't
sit still. My mama say I'm special... and that's
why... I'm in Special Education. The teacher
taught me how to, how to get in line and shut up.
Yeah, that's how I knew I didn't need school
because I already knew how to get in the welfare
line and shut up when the police is talkin' to
me.

*If a kid's daily diet consists of junk food and Top Ramen, we
should not be surprised when that kid struggles in school or is
misdiagnosed with some type of learning disability. Parents please
make sure your child is eating, resting and exercising properly
before you put them on any "legal" drugs or into any "special"
programs. It didn't take long for DeMariay to deem his school
education useless.*

Bubblin' to the surface, drippin' from my lips
like vomited venom. This is the vernacular of a
virgin who has never known love, but fucks the
world everyday, in every way. And if you wanted
your car stereo then you shoulda' kept the doors
locked. And if you wanted your laptop then you
shouldn't have brought it with you. And if you
didn't want me to rape you, then you shouldn't
have been home when I broke in. Or better yet,
bitch, you shouldn't have let the world rape me.
So fuck you!

*By the end of DeMariay's monologue, he is a lost soul and blames
society for his predicament. What follows is his forfeiture of a
future along with a disturbing rationalization of evil. He
unfortunately justifies his violations in the present and future, by
blaming those that violated him in the past.*

Dawn Williams Ferreira, Ph.D. and Jinho "The Piper" Ferreira

# EARLE WASHINGTON

*Earle Washington hates everything, and everybody.*
*He hates his community. He hates the fact that his older sister got killed and his younger sister is a drug addict. He hates the killers, drug dealers, and the prostitutes that hide their secrets.*

*He hates the parents that don't help their children with their homework and only show up in school when their child is failing. He hates the teachers that don't know the first thing about their students' realities, don't attempt to know, and wonder why their students are failing. He hates the therapists that attempt to "correct" the black student's behavior without knowing anything about black history, black culture, or how their little black 'project' fits into a structurally white world.*

*He hates the protesters, who are often those same parents, teachers, and therapists that protest him for arresting/beating the shit out of/killing their former black 'project' because none of them did their job properly.*

*He hates that being an ignorant rapper or video ho' is some children's highest aspirations.*

*He hates the random black person that rolls his eyes at him as he drives by in his police car.*

*He hates the crowd of people filming him with their cell phones while he's detaining a murder suspect at gunpoint.*

*He hates that 23-month-old Hiram Lawrence got shot in the head and killed in front of over 20 people yet nobody saw anything.*

*He hates that 3-year-old Carlos Nava got shot in the neck and killed in broad daylight as his family pushed him in a stroller.*

*He hates that 5-year-old Gabriel Martínez was shot and killed while his family's taco truck was being robbed.*

*He hates that 8-year-old Alaysha Carradine got murdered and only 40 people showed up to the candlelight vigil days after thousands poured into the streets to protest the Trayvon Martin verdict.*

*He hates that people who look like him killed Hiram, Carlos, Gabriel and Alaysha.*

*He hates that he receives a weekly police bulletin that on average contains over 20 black mules wanted for murder and robbery and almost half of them are wearing black "hoodies." He hates that one of last week's attempted murder suspects is 12- years old.*

*He hates the black people that hate him because he's a cop. He hates the white cops that hate him because he's a cop.*

*He hates talk radio because they talk too fucking much.*

*He hates the Crips and the Bloods because they killed more black people in Los Angeles in the 1980's than the Ku Klux Klan has killed since 1882.*

*He hates black intellectuals because when they hear statistics like the one previously mentioned they either deny their validity or just blame white supremacy.*

*He hates the rappers that taught the world how to Crip walk. He hates the rappers that made being a Blood cool. He hates the radio because it plays music about killing and pimping black people at 7 AM when he's taking his son to school.*

*He hates the fact that if the radio played music created by the Ku Klux Klan about killing black people, black intellectuals and black Crip and Blood rappers would lose their minds.*

*He hates the fact that if most of these rappers weren't making millions rapping about selling drugs to, killing and pimping black people, they would probably be doing it. He hates that he's torn between being proud of them and wanting to kill them.*

*He hates the fact that George Zimmerman knows ain't nobody gon' do shit about him killing Trayvon Martin but write raps and spoken word pieces – unless, of course, George Zimmerman goes to prison.*

*He hates so-called revolutionary rappers because it seems as if the majority of their fans are affluent, highly educated white people. He hates affluent, highly educated white people because they do shit like go to Zimbabwe and Sierra Leone to volunteer when there are kids being murdered across the street from their condos.*

*He hates conservatives, liberals and progressives because he just held a dead baby in his arms and all they want to talk about is drones, abortion and gay rights.*

*Earle Washington has no sense of global economics or global politics. While growing up he spent his afternoons stealing dinner from the liquor store or running errands for his older sister's drug-dealing boyfriends. He has never heard of Robert Reich and cannot make the connection between Wall Street, IMF lending practices, and the dead baby he's holding in his arms. His focus is on the baby's drug-dealing father who ironically survived the shooting. He hates HIM.*

*I'm sure somewhere in all of this, Earle probably even hates himself.*

# DEMARIAY MCDANIELS
# AND EARLE WASHINGTON

*DeMariay McDaniels and Earle Washington are from the same community, and they hate it equally. Both come from broken homes, have lost family members to violence or addiction, and are plagued with PTSD.*

*DeMariay victimizes the weak of the community without conscience. As far as he understands, this is just the order of things. As a child he was victimized by the strong, now it is simply his turn to be the strong victimizing others.*

*Earle escaped the trappings of the inner city in his late teens when his family moved to the suburbs. But by then it was too late. His oldest sister had already been killed in a shooting meant for her drug-dealing boyfriend. His younger sister had already become a crack addict occasionally prostituting herself for the next fix. Earle's hatred for the community had already been solidified by the time he escaped it.*

*While the horrors of the inner city deeply affect both DeMariay and Earle, their lives take drastically different paths only to once again find themselves reunited in the abandoned auto-plant (which serves as a symbol of the death of the black middle class).*

*Their lives end in that reunification; DeMariay is murdered, Earle sets into motion a series of events ending in his being found guilty of murder.*

*Since Earle killed DeMariay for pimping his niece, he might be considered a vigilante and possibly a hero but the fact that he is a police officer complicates the issue. I wanted to challenge my audience to think outside of their preconceived notions of right and wrong.*

FIVE

# AWAKENING POSSIBILITIES

*Cops and Robbers* is prolific.  In many ways, it became a resume for Piper's creativity, communication skills, way of seeing different perspectives, and way of thinking differently about finding solutions. This made him stand out to certain supervisors in ACSO.  One of them was Lieutenant Marty Neideffer, the founder of the Deputy Sheriffs' Activities League (DSAL).  When he saw the play, he knew that Piper would be an asset to his team. Neideffer is a part of the struggle within policing that involves shifting from law enforcement to public safety and working at a more preventative and restorative level.  This can be translated to a prioritization of youth and ex-offenders.

No longer working in the jails and having successfully passed the arduous Field Training Officer (FTO) program, Piper is now a deputy sheriff in the DSAL unit stationed at the Recreation, Education, Arts, Career, and Health (REACH) Ashland Community Center. In this capacity, he works on developing projects that focus on crime prevention and countering recidivism which allow him to employ his creativity in policing.
At the center in the Ashland area of unincorporated Alameda County, DSAL leads the recreation. The $25 million state-of-the-art building houses among other amenities, a studio, a library, a wellness center, and a childcare facility. The center provides services for youth between the ages of 11-24.

Piper, along with other deputies, line the streets with their vehicles to make sure that children leave school and arrive at the REACH Ashland Community Center without being shot, robbed, or kidnapped as part of Operation Safe Passage.

After school, REACH is packed. Respect for this space reflects off of the graffiti-free bathroom walls. Young people are receiving mental and physical health services, finding out job information, reading books, and participating in fitness, music, art, and creative writing programs. Five days a week deputies volunteer their time to teach youth boxing, and Piper has formed a young men's group called "Pen and Sword" where young men are pushed to their limits physically and mentally. The DSAL unit coordinates a plethora of activities ranging from a soccer league that serves 1300 youth to a rites of passage course.

On a weekly basis, Piper and other deputies create an open and honest space for youth to ask questions regarding public safety. Discussions have spanned subjects including crimes involving juveniles, racial profiling, and a history of law enforcement in the black community. The youth have been asked on occasion to describe what they believe law enforcement should be. Piper says more often than not, the discussions have become a learning experience for deputies as well as the youth

Knowing that many young people have been conditioned to want to make money quickly, Piper created a program called "Smart Money." He provides the youth with a legitimate way to earn $20 in 20 minutes, while celebrating intelligence. Youngsters take a timed test with English and math questions from standardized exams. The student with the most correct answers wins the money and receives tremendous public recognition from the youth center. Local businesses have caught on to the success of the program and have donated funds for "Smart Money."

Another strategy in protecting the community is to positively affect the people coming out of jail. In order to counter the underground economy based on drug dealing and prostitution, ex-offenders need alternative employment. Dig Deep Farms Social Enterprise, a business run by a non-profit, creates a healthy product for the community and employs people who have formerly been incarcerated. Dig Deep provides job opportunities in an area where the unemployment rate surpasses the national average. This hands-on approach also provides a solution to Bay Area food deserts, making low-cost, organic fruits and vegetables available to the community. When Piper visits the farm he rolls up his sleeves and gets dirty.  He may have seen some of the ex-offenders in jail at one time but titles disappear when working side-by-side doing manual labor. These men are no longer inmates; they are working men being paid a livable wage.

With Soulciety, a non-profit that provides training and employment for youth, Piper, along with other ACSO deputies invested an entire summer into finding businesses in the area that would look past a youth's criminal record when hiring.  In this partnership, deputies are vouching for ex-juvenile offenders, and allowing them the opportunity to make positive change for themselves.

As an Oakland native, Piper is a reflection of the people from the community who have an unquantifiable love, trust, talent, and commitment to working toward change.  He knows people who are invested in the community, like he is, in their work with youth and ex-offenders.  Piper builds on the connections that he has established and seeks out people who have been doing work that is empowering the community yet often goes unrecognized or underfunded.  He strategically looks for ways to leverage the resources of the sheriff's office to assist individuals and organizations that battle to save our youth and provide options to locking people up.

Piper's new position calls for being able to shift gears from being an instructor or counselor to a negotiator to activating as a street cop on a daily basis. He has literally had to walk out of class on more than one occasion to assist in tracking down a robbery or attempted murder suspect. Not only are the actual programs a way to prevent children from going to jail and bring restorative justice, Piper is a part of a shift in policing strategies. When officers engage people with a public safety versus a law enforcement mentality they are guided by the premise that they are helping people to make their neighborhoods safer. Piper has even answered 9-1-1 calls that turned out to be mothers who needed assistance with their sons. IIc would find himself standing by a mother and providing consequences for a young male who did not want to listen. Piper is a community male role model and he knows how to speak to people. I have no doubt that the people he deals with get exactly what they deserve because his style of policing comes from a place of community love.

Because working in this realm is at the cutting edge for deputy sheriffs, it requires imagination, ingenuity, and flexibility. For this reason, Neideffer feels that Piper is a perfect fit for this program. On the subject of what Piper brings to the table, Neideffer told me, "I don't quite know yet. He's a unique guy, a unique deputy with a unique skill set that I am still learning about. He's a remarkable guy and I don't quite know how to go beyond that. You know better than I do about where his potential lies outside of the industry, but he's a strong guy and he could influence the trajectory of law enforcement if he was to stay in it."

Piper remains humble and knows he has a lot to learn when it comes to the art of policing. He describes the profession as, "multidimensional with the capacity of exploding from tedious to dynamic within seconds." Piper says that he has met deputies who live for the art and has been mentored by some of the best ACSO has to offer. Theirs is a culture of refinement—spending off-days studying policy, training, or at the shooting range. Some of their styles he agrees with, others not so much, but he places learning before making friends.

As a cop, Piper awakens possibilities. My husband's experience has shown me that he is not the only one wearing a badge that cares deeply about black youth. Because I know that we need an increase in positive male role models for our youth, I imagine what it would be like if Piper were able to take an army of his brothers with him to enroll in the police academy. If our community's fathers and uncles were the police, would we be more proud and accepting of our public safety officers? Would talking to the police feel more like getting help than snitching? If we knew that we had selected our best and brightest warriors to protect us, would our community be more forgiving when they had to use force?

As a playwright, Piper shakes up our sensibilities. After viewing *Cops and Robbers*, inspired audience members have posed the question, "What actions can I take?" Below, we have come up with a few suggestions that are reflective of Piper's public safety and my education background.

1. Publicize the positive things that are happening in your community.
2. Support organizations that support the youth and ex-offenders.
3. Police your community with a public safety mentality.
4. Create opportunities for apprenticeship.
5. Get people to see *Cops and Robbers* and use the following curriculum to process the play with someone.

# COPS AND ROBBERS CURRICULUM
By Dawn Williams Ferreira, Ph.D.

The first time I saw my husband's play was when I was seven months pregnant with our daughter. It was Piper's first debut to a small group of family and friends. Previously, between the months of March and June, Piper had written and memorized *Cops and Robbers* sharing the project only with his former acting teacher Ami Zins and her husband Lew Levinson who were the directors. He accomplished all of this while working full-time as a deputy sheriff.

As he was writing his play, I was finishing my dissertation on post-traumatic stress disorder in urban schools. The two of us typically share everything with each other but our arduous travails on our individual projects meant often working apart. Yet, from the moment I saw the play I recognized the connections between my husband's play and my dissertation and the reflections of our own real life experiences. As he grappled with the idea of black people on both sides of the law, I looked at mental health issues among adolescents and teachers in urban classroom settings. *Cops and Robbers* brought us together professionally. It led to the creation of our family business, Pipedreamz Entertainment, a space where both of our fields of expertise complement each other.

I am an educator. As a teacher with over a dozen years of experience, I have taught in public schools both in the U.S. and abroad. I have run into my former students throughout my community and even at UC Berkeley where they were undergraduates and I was a graduate student. I have also endured the pain of attending funerals for my students. Some of my students have gone to jail and come into contact with my husband.

Piper is a griot. He is an outstanding storyteller. From tucking our children in at night with imaginary bedtime adventures to doing impersonations from movies, he has always impressed me with his uncanny ability to bring characters to life. I often told him that he needed to do a one-man show but when he did, I had no idea what to expect.

Watching his one-man play *Cops and Robbers* is a unique visual and audio experience. This is far from a feel-good movie where everyone leaves feeling that all is right in the world but rather a show that calls everyone out—no one is safe—and shakes up the status quo. It is the most honest and most intelligent theatrical piece I have ever seen and I am convinced that he is the only person on Earth who could have executed this play. He possesses the dynamic combination of being a creative artist, a law enforcement officer, and an Oakland native. The story line masterfully unfolds revealing a complex cast of 17 characters representing the media, law enforcement, and the community, all of whom are played by Piper.

However, this play is more than entertainment. Piper has created transformative art that inspires audience members to think and act in a way that positively affects their communities. This curriculum serves as a tool for educators, mentors, and parents to collectively process with youth before seeing the play and to facilitate discussions generated after viewing *Cops and Robbers*. However, it should be recognized that the issues raised in *Cops and Robbers* are of a sensitive nature. Piper is dealing with commercial sexual exploitation of children, gun violence, the media, the community, and law enforcement. It is important to note that the people who watch this play, including our youth, may be triggered by the content. The following chart Figure 1. drawn from my dissertation, *Healing Lessons: Urban High School Teachers Learning to Teach Black Youth with Post-Traumatic Stress Disorder* shows the manifestations of PTSD in the classroom.

## Figure 1. Manifestations of PTSD in the Classroom

| Criteria for PTSD in DSM-IV-TR | Symptoms of PTSD | Manifestations in class |
| --- | --- | --- |
| Intrusive recollections | Nightmares | Exhaustion, sleep-deprivation |
| | Feelings that relive traumatic experiences, anxiety | Need to self-soothe, self-medication, thumb sucking, clinginess to teacher |
| Avoidance / Numbing | Feelings of hopelessness, worthlessness | Giving up, dropping out, not putting effort into work, poor decision-making |
| | Efforts to avoid associations with trauma | Not coming to class, laughing at inappropriate times |
| | Detachment from others, isolation | Difficulty with group work and collaboration |
| | Recall difficulties | Difficulty with memorizing information that seems irrelevant to survival |
| | Dissociation, zoning out | Not paying attention in class |
| | No longer enjoying activities that brought enjoyment | Not coming to class |
| Generalized hyper-arousal | Somatization, stomach pain, headaches | Missing class |
| | Inability to modulate sexual impulses | Harassing of peers, teachers; inappropriate conduct |
| Release of norepinephrine in brain | Cognitive processing of language | Struggles with literacy, difficulty putting thoughts into words, preference for art |
| | | (Continued) |

109

| Criteria for PTSD in DSM-IV-TR | Symptoms of PTSD | Manifestations in class |
|---|---|---|
| Hyper-arousal | Insomnia | Exhaustion, sleep-deprivation |
| | Irritability | Difficulty working with others, bullying, issues resolving conflict, lack of respect for authority |
| | Angry outbursts | Disruptive behaviors, fighting |
| | Difficulty concentrating | Unfocused, difficulty doing work |
| | Hyper-vigilance | Lack of trust in others, walking around the classroom, wanting to sit by the door, not wanting to sit in a seating chart |

©2013 Williams Ferreira

Student reactions can range. One student might completely shut down, while another engages in comical distractions. It is vital that the educator or parent engaging youth with this curriculum is prepared for the different emotions and reactions and attempts to provide a safe space for them.

Perspective, Growth, Awareness, Dignity, and Power are the titles of the sections under which each lesson plan falls. Not only are these titles but values that are intentionally the focus of each section. Teachers and guardians should feel free to define these principles with young people and generate discussion about how these values apply to their lives. I suggest that each person who participates in the lesson plans record entries into a journal or blog. Art is a therapeutic outlet and artistic expression in various forms such as drawing, music, and acting should be encouraged.

# USING THIS CURRICULUM

Coding is used to differentiate lesson plans that can support before or after viewing the play. Activities marked with one asterisk "*" are best used before watching the play. Two asterisks "**" indicate that the activity is best reserved for after seeing the play. If there are three asterisks, "***" the activity can be done either before or after the play. It is advised that educators preview the script and the curriculum so that they can be acquainted with the content. Activities are written with the idea that educators need leeway in developing their own lesson plans to tailor fit standards and their class curriculum. It is my hope that the lesson plan suggestions can be implemented in ways that accentuate what teachers already have in place. I invite anyone who uses this curriculum to fill out the survey at the end as well.

It is with gratitude, that I address the teachers, mentors, and guardians who will engage in bold dialogues and take courageous action with their youth inspired by this play.

# PERSPECTIVE

Before watching the play *Cops and Robbers*, students should understand that this theatrical piece is a one-person play. The actor Piper peels layers off of a complicated story that deals with gun violence, commercial sexual exploitation of youth, law enforcement, and the media. Portraying different characters, Piper looks at a single news event from 17 points of view.

**Understanding point of view***
The following New York Times article: http://www.nytimes.com/1994/04/13/us/laughter-at-film-brings-spielberg-visit.html tells the story of a high school field trip where students laughed during a violent scene in a movie about the Jewish Holocaust. As students read the article have them pick out the various people mentioned and have them note the various perspectives on the incident. After reading the article and discussing the significance, students can look up other related articles about the incident that help them understand the different points of view. Have students select 3-5 characters (such as a student, a news reporter, an audience member, the movie theater manager, a parent/guardian, a teacher, or a fly on the wall, etc.) and write their sides of the story. Who would they select and why? What would the selected characters say and why? Accompany each write-up with a drawing of what students imagine the characters to look like.

***pre-play activity **post-play activity ***either before or after the play**

**Next Level*****
Allow students the opportunity to act out the various characters
they have selected in the activity above. Doing impersonations of
different people means noting particular nuances of each character.
Is there a particular way that a person stands or speaks? What
props would they need? For example, a student might put a pencil
behind an ear to characterize a teacher or hold it up like a
microphone to portray the news reporter. How can a story be
communicated through the eyes of others?

**Being a Member***
What does it mean to be a member of an audience, a class, a team,
or a community? What types of rules are followed in each
scenario? Why are these rules put into place? What happens when
these rules are not followed? After students have read the New
York Times article found at:
http://www.nytimes.com/1994/04/13/us/laughter-at-film-brings-
spielberg-visit.html, done the writing activity above, and possibly
tried their hand at performing their own one-person shows, have
students explore the feelings of being on stage, being in the
audience, and being scandalized nationally as a young person.

***pre-play activity **post-play activity ***either before or after the play**

# GROWTH

*Cops and Robbers* begins with a monologue from an African ancestor speaking as if he is watching over the world in its current state. In the play's opening line the African elder explains, "...a boy could not become a man just because he had his birthday." He emphasizes becoming strong men and women because they are seen as producing strong children, thus continuing a legacy. The African ancestor says that those who used and took advantage of other people were considered parasites and removed from the village.

**Adulthood***
Allow each student time to brainstorm what it means to be an adult. Have students work in pairs to refine their definitions. Bring the whole class together and see if the class can agree on a definition for what it means to be an adult. How did the class develop the definition? Is there a link to laws, education, puberty, etc.? What do students think about the banishment of people who take advantage of others from their village? How would this compare to incarceration?

**Rites of Passage***
Prof. Manu Ampim provides details on the African initiation process for becoming an adult in this article found at: http://www.manuampim.com/AfricanInitiationRites.htm. Allow students research time to investigate how people in other cultures define becoming an adult and the celebrations that take place. Have students present their findings. How do these traditions compare to the definitions of what it means to be an adult from the previous activity? Why do these rituals take place? What does it mean to give up these rituals? Do students feel that there is honor in growing older? Why or why not?

***pre-play activity **post-play activity ***either before or after the play**

**Forever Young*****

At http://www.manuampim.com/AfricanInitiationRites.htm, Prof. Manu Ampim explains that in African culture, rituals and celebrations exist for births, becoming an adult, marriage, becoming an elder, and death. How does American culture contrast with African culture in embodying the idea of "forever young"? Have students look through magazines and see if they find ads for products that assist in preserving youthfulness. How is the idea of staying young reflected in hip-hop? How many hip-hop artists can students name with Young, Li'l, or anything reflecting the idea of youth in their titles? Can they create their own versions of ads that celebrate growing older?

**Making Ancestors Proud*****

Allow students to research their families and the ancestors from which they descend. What ideas and values did they espouse? How far back do students know their family history? Have students imagine that they have descended from royalty and one of their ancestors has accompanied them for an entire week. How would students walk? What would the ancestor see? What would their ancestors think about the current state of the world? How would students explain the state of the world to an ancestor? Have students write themselves letters from their ancestors' points of view giving them advice about their lives and their futures.

***pre-play activity **post-play activity ***either before or after the play**

# AWARENESS

Two of the characters in *Cops and Robbers*, Emma Insti'gator and Rob Bob, are representatives of the media. Emma Insti'gator's character is the reporter who races for the leading news story and thrives on controversy because she is trying to further her career in journalism. Rob Bob is an opinionated conservative radio talk show host. The characters come to life in a way that inspires critical media literacy.

**Listen Up*****
As a class, listen to, watch, or read various sources of news. Pick some conservative, liberal, and progressive programs. What messages do you hear? What values are being discussed in each program? Who are the sponsors and advertisers that fund each show? What is similar and different about them? Break students up into groups based on top news stories and have students analyze the perspective that each news program takes in presenting the top stories. What images are shown? How are they presented? Challenge students to spark up conversations about the news with at least three people outside of the classroom and note their comments, opinions, and typical news sources.

**Nothing but the Truth*****
Emma Insti'gator chases down police officers and community members to get the full story. What clues do students use to determine that a source is reliable, particularly when conducting research online? What tactics do news reporters employ to portray a believable story? How do you know what the truth is?

***pre-play activity **post-play activity ***either before or after the play**

**Economic Effects*****

In the play, an old auto plant is the setting for the altercation between the police officer and the civilian. Emma Insti'gator says it "once employed thousands of Oakland residents." What is the link between economics and the current state of crime in the United States? Have students create a chart that illustrates the effect of the employment rate on the crime rate? Have students generate a list of jobs and careers based on the play. Then have them rank them in order of importance in society.  They can work individually at first, then in pairs, and then in groups.

**Up For Debate****

Among many memorable lines, Rob Bob complains, "...all of your little barefooted, teachers' unions wanna keep pumping more and more of our tax payer dollars into schools that are failing and libraries that nobody down there even utilizes." In his opinion more money should go to law enforcement. Have students brainstorm other controversial topics based on some of Rob Bob's rants or current news items and stage informal debates. Create a space where students feel compelled to read the news in order to stay updated on current events. Have students try arguing both sides of an issue. Students can also get into character as they debate, trying their acting skills as Rob Bob.

***pre-play activity **post-play activity ***either before or after the play**

# DIGNITY

*Cops and Robbers* delves into the issues of dehumanization and the commercial sexual exploitation of children whose innocence and dignity are stolen. Piper portrays a pimp who describes sexual exploitation in an unadulterated manner. This scene is a critical piece in the play and the monologue is powerful to hear because it is a single voice. His nefarious acts are exposed and there is no background music or song lyric to glamorize his behavior. Students should be aware of the many constant forces in their lives attacking their dignity and self-respect.

**Dollars and Innocence*****
Youth advocates are trying to replace the term "teenage prostitution" with commercial sexually exploited children (CSEC). What is the difference between these terms? What is connoted by the term "teenage" versus "children"? And "commercial sexually exploited" versus "prostitution"? Have students define the terms, research the facts and laws, and create a chart for the arrest rate/sentencing of: a.) a CSEC b.) an adult prostitute c.) a pimp d.) a john. What does this chart reveal about the justice system? Were there any surprises? In economics, it is taught that supply is based on demand. How does this apply to sex trafficking? Why are street hustlers switching from drug dealing to sexual exploitation? What is a "john school"? For more information, here is a link to a "john school" article: http://www.pbs.org/now/shows/422/prostitution.html and other resources. How many sexually trafficked victims are killed? What are the rates of infection for sexually trafficked victims?

***pre-play activity **post-play activity ***either before or after the play**

**Pimp Culture*****

Pimp culture is representative of the wounds of slavery. White slave owners raped black women and girls. After slavery ended, black men exercised power and control over women to profit off of male sexual desires. (See Prof. Beth Coleman's "Pimp Notes on Autonomy" and former pimp Iceberg Slim's books where he recounts psychological exploits.) Pimps, similar to slave owners, employ dehumanizing practices in the name of capitalism. The dehumanization and violation of women and children has become widely glorified in the mainstream. Can students name examples of pimp culture used in television, music, movies, etc.? What dehumanizing practices do other businesses employ? How are these practices glorified in mainstream media?

**Hypocrisy and Humanization*****

Marc Dub, a pimp from the play describes a sexually trafficked minor being killed yet says that he would not allow someone to pimp his own niece. Are students familiar with other examples of people whose words might contradict their actions? What makes one life more valuable than another? How does a person "humanize" others or see them as people and not objects? Have students brainstorm at what point treatment of other people is considered less than humane? Students can look up the United Nations Rights of a Child at: http://www.unicef.org/crc/index_30177.html particularly focusing on protection rights.

***pre-play activity **post-play activity ***either before or after the play**

**Father Figures*****

In the play *Cops and Robbers,* one character is a pimp who describes young women as needing "a foot on their neck" and someone to call "Daddy." Like slave owners who fathered many of their slaves through rape, how do pimps' violence and sexual exploitation of women relate to an unhealthy father figure? What are the characteristics of a good father figure? Another pimp in the play says that his father was "everybody and nobody." What does this mean? How could relationships with fathers contribute to becoming a pimp or being sexually exploited? How could relationships with fathers contribute to the way that people relate to authority figures in general?

**Peer-to-Peer****

Have students check out pieces that were written by youth. A Youth Radio investigative report found at: http://www.npr.org/2010/12/06/131757019/youth-radio-trafficked-teen-girls-describe-life-in-the-game on teenage sex trafficking features young women who have left and survived commercial sexual exploitation. Also, visit the Motivating, Inspiring, Supporting, and Serving Sexually Exploited Youth site (http://www.misssey.org ) where students can find links to resources and creative writing written by youth, including 10 Things I Would Tell A Twelve- Year-Old Girl Who Was In "The Life". Students can embark on a letter-writing campaign to youth who are currently being commercial sexually exploited. Before writing, students should read the Bay Area Women Against Rape (http://www.bawar.org ) page on Helping Survivors of Sexual Assault Letters can be sent to BAWAR Attn. Pat Mims 470 27th St. Oakland, CA 94612 or another local place of safety for sexually trafficked youth. The letters can be brief, positive, decorated messages of advice, encouragement, or a fact/statistic about sexual exploitation. It is advised that students sign only their first names or keep them anonymous. Students can additionally organize donations for organizations such as MISSSEY or BAWAR.


***pre-play activity **post-play activity ***either before or after the play**

120

# POWER

*Cops and Robbers* brings up many of the issues that can affect people in highly stressed neighborhoods. The stress of living around constant mental, emotional, and physical abuse either experienced firsthand or witnessing it among others can take a toll on one's health and wellbeing. It is important to have an understanding of the historical roots of problems in order to understand how to solve them and claim one's power.

### Self-Control*
Because this section is about power begin by teaching a breathing technique that shows students that they have control over themselves. Explain that this is a tool they can use for stress. Have students sit in a powerfully straight position. Breathe in for four counts. Hold for four counts. Breathe out for four counts. Hold for four counts. Repeat four times. Challenge the class to sit up straight in the power stance for the entire class. While watching the play, if there are any triggering moments, students can use this breathing technique.

### Black Death***
One of the main characters, Earle Washington says, "And as a matter of fact, the Crips have killed more black people than the Ku Klux Klan did." Is this a true statement? Do the research to find out the actual numbers and create a chart. What are students' thoughts about this? Conduct research on your neighborhood. What types of crimes take place? Who are the victims? Who are the perpetrators? Do the police officers reflect the ethnic make-up of the population?

***pre-play activity **post-play activity ***either before or after the play**

## Sick Wit' It[1]**

Post-traumatic stress disorder commonly affects soldiers who return home from war and law enforcement officers because they have been traumatized by violence. Similarly, many people who grow up in highly stressed neighborhoods are also affected by traumatic situations yet go undiagnosed. Students can read more about PTSD at: http://www.nimh.nih.gov/health/publications/post-traumatic-stress-disorder-ptsd/index.shtml. Being exposed to physical and emotional trauma on a frequent basis puts community members at risk for complex PTSD. People such as paramedics, therapists, teachers, and others who work closely with traumatized people can be prone to vicarious traumatization, developing emotional and physical reactions from absorbing the painful experiences of others.

What are some elements of a highly stressed neighborhood that can cause PTSD? What are some of the symptoms of PTSD? How are manifestations of PTSD in soldiers who return from war similar and different from those who are traumatized from surviving life-threatening situations in their own communities? Have students imagine that they are therapists. Using this lens, which characters in the play would they diagnose with PTSD? Complex PTSD? Vicarious traumatization? Which ones do they think are not suffering? What informed their thought process? What are some local organizations that provide services?

---

[1] Dr. Joy DeGruy connects many of the struggles of Black people today with slavery, terming it Post-Traumatic Slave Syndrome (PTSS).
***pre-play activity **post-play activity ***either before or after the play**

**Self-Medication****

One of the most common ways of dealing with PTSD is substance abuse. Two of the main characters in the play, Marc Dub and Earle Washington, abuse substances during their monologues. This tactic brings out the rawness of their stories and shows them self-medicating their own trauma. What are some of the stressors that have come up for these characters throughout the play? What examples of glamorized self-medication can students find in popular culture? What are some alternative remedies for symptoms of PTSD?

**Who You Callin' a Snitch?*****

Since slavery, snitching in the black community has a history of being the ultimate betrayal of an unspoken unity that black people developed during a time when freedom, voting, and literacy were illegal yet black people could legally be raped. This solidarity was disrupted whenever a black person told white authority figures if other black people broke plantation rules. Can students think of other historical times when snitching was used to destroy solidarity? In present times is snitching still considered disloyal? Marc Dub makes the distinction between a "'hood" situation ("I ain't seen nothin', I ain't heard nothin'") and a police situation ("somebody gotta say something"). Where do students see examples of black unity today? How is black unity disrupted when black people commit crimes against each other? Ayah Young's article: http://www.wiretapmag.org/race/43473/ provides information and helpful links about informing, including links to Rick Frei's Snitching Project and intersections with hip-hop.

***pre-play activity **post-play activity ***either before or after the play**

**Cops and Robbers****
The Minister's character is the voice of historical consciousness. He says, "Brothers and sisters, I am here to remind you that should we all bow our heads, and look at the ground beneath our feet...we would be looking at the land that was *robbed* away from our brothers and sisters, the Native Americans. Should we look into the eyes of each other...we would be looking into the faces of the children that were, *robbed* away from our one true motherland, the great continent of Africa." How does this excerpt from the Minister's speech and the play's content help to explain the meaning of the play's title?

**Peace, Love, and Books****
Piper first wrote this play in March of 2012. His character Rob Bob who uses baseless exaggerations to make his points says, "And by the way...the libraries are open. But the crime rate is so high that you gotta shoot your way into 'em. And God help you, may lord Jesus Christ bless you, if you forget to bring enough ammo to shoot your way back out." Though Rob Bob's words may seem like a hyperbole, Caitlin Esch, wrote an article found at: http://blogs.kqed.org/newsfix/2013/02/21/second-and-third-graders-protest-gun-violence/ a year later, in February 2013 with a photo gallery about a similar topic. Have students read her article and check out the images. How does Esch's article compare to Rob Bob's comments? What stands out most to students about this piece? How is this an example of the multiple lives that can be affected by gun violence? What assets do students recognize in their own communities? In what ways do students stand up for what is right and claim their power? Similar to Piper, have students experienced the power of writing something that came true? How can the ideas that students envision and write down manifest in a positive way? Also see Marsha Rhynes' *Write to Live: Telling our Stories* as an example of a teacher who has empowered her students to write the stories of their lives and published their narratives in a collection.

***pre-play activity **post-play activity ***either before or after the play**

**Empowerment****

DeMariay McDaniel's soliloquy (p.38) describes being violated by the world and putting his feelings of voicelessness and powerlessness into victimizing others. He talks about his family and being raised by his grandmother because neither of his parents was around.  DeMariay also mentions his connections to incarceration, education, nutrition, health care, and law enforcement. At the end of his monologue, he screams, "You shouldn't have let the world rape me," as justification for his own nefarious behavior. What are the problems that DeMariay raises and how do these issues play into this young man's life? How can change be made in the various institutions he mentions? At the same time, how can DeMariay be held accountable for his actions? Have students write letters or perform a monologue addressed to DeMariay, his mother, his father, his grandmother, a political official, a peer, or anyone that they can relate to in order to convey a message of societal solutions.

***pre-play activity **post-play activity ***either before or after the play**

# SURVEY

**These questions are to be answered after the play has been viewed. Please email your responses to: copsandrobbersplay@gmail.com.**

**Who were the most memorable characters?**

**Which character could you relate to most and why?**

**What, if any, new perspectives about law enforcement did the play offer?**

**What, if any, new perspectives about the media did the play offer?**

**What, if any, new perspectives about people of African descent did the play offer?**

**What do you think the judge's sentence was at the end of the play? Why?**

**What has the play inspired you to do for yourself and your community?**

**What specific activities in the curriculum helped in processing the play? Why?**

**Would you recommend this play to a friend? Why?**

# BIBLIOGRAPHY


Alexander, M. (2010). *A new Jim Crow: Mass incarceration in the age of colorblindness.* New York, NY: New Press

Ampim, M. (2003, September). *Africana studies: The five major African initiation rites.* Retrieved May 7, 2013, from http://www.manuampim.com/AfricanInitiationRites.htm

Artz, M., Neysa, N., & Mejia, B. (2013, July 18). Oakland 8-year old shot dead at sleepover. *San José Mercury.* Retrieved August 16, 2013, from http://www.mercurynews.com/ci_23689305/oakland-8-year-old-shot-dead-at-sleepover

Blackmon, D. A. (2008). *Slavery by another name: the re-enslavement of black Americans from the Civil War to World War II.* New York, NY: Random House

Chalmers, D. M. (1981). *Hooded Americanism: A history of the Ku Klux Klan.* Durham, NC: Duke University Press

Coleman, B. (2003). Pimp notes on autonomy. In Tate, G. (Ed.) *Everything but the burden: What white people are taking from black culture.* New York, NY: Broadway Books

Collins, T. (2011, December 9). Hiram Lawrence, Oakland Toddler In Rap Video Shooting, Dies. *Huffington Post.* Retrieved August 16, 2013, from http://www.huffingtonpost.com/2011/12/09/hiram-lawrence-oakland-to_n_1140345.html?

Davis, M. (1990). *City of quartz: Excavating the future of Los Angeles.* New York, NY: Verso.

De Gruy, J. (2005). *Post-traumatic slave syndrome: America's legacy of injury and healing.* Milwaukie, OR: Uptone Press.

Dulaney, W. M. (1996). *Black police in America*. Bloomington, IN: Indiana University Press.

Esch, C. (2013, February 21). Oakland students march to protest gun violence. *KQED*. Retrieved May 7, 2013, from http://blogs.kqed.org/newsfix/2013/02/21/second-and-third-graders-protest-gun-violence/

Ferreira, D.L.C.W (2012) *Healing lessons: Urban high school teachers learning to teach black youth with post-traumatic stress disorder*. (Doctoral dissertation). Retrieved from ProQuest Dissertations and Theses. (Accession Order No. AAT 3527125)

Goldhaber, M. H. (1992). Attention: The system of post-Industrialism? *Z papers*. 1( 2). (April-June)

John schools. (2008, May 30). John schools: Can men who hire prostitutes be reformed? *PBS*. Retrieved May 7, 2013, from http://www.pbs.org/now/shows/422/prostitution.html

Jones, C. & Lee, H. K. (2011, August 10). Oakland mourns 3-year-old Carlos Nava's slaying. *San Francisco Chronicle*. Retrieved August 16, 2013, from http://www.sfgate.com/bayarea/article/Oakland-mourns-3-year-old-Carlos-Nava-s-slaying-2335633.php

Lagos, M. & Lee, H. K. (2012, January 1). Oakland boy shot near family's taco truck dies. *San Francisco Chronicle*. Retrieved August 16, 2013, from http://www.sfgate.com/crime/article/Oakland-boy-shot-near-family-s-taco-truck-dies-2434480.php

Lakoff, G. (2003). California budget crisis caused by 'minority rule.' Retrieved August 16, 2013, from http://fora.tv/2009/08/03/Politics_of_Language_George_Lakoff/California_Budget_Crisis_Caused_by_Minority_Rule

Laughter at Film. (Anonymous, 1994, April 13). Laughter at film brings Spielberg visit. *New York Times.* Retrieved May 7, 2013, from http://www.nytimes.com/1994/04/13/us/laughter-at-film-brings-spielberg-visit.html

"Lynchings: by year and race," statistics. Date unknown. Tuskegee Institute Archives. Retrieved May 7, 2012, from http://law2.umkc.edu/faculty/projects/ftrials/shipp/lynchingyear.html

National Institute of Mental Health. (2010, January 1). *Post-traumatic stress disorder (PTSD).* Retrieved May 7, 2013, from http://www.nimh.nih.gov/health/publications/post-traumatic-stress-disorder-ptsd/index.shtml

Newton, H. (1973). *Revolutionary Suicide.* New York, NY: Penguin Group

Robinson, E. (2010). *Disintegration: The splintering of black America.* New York, NY: Random House

Rhynes, M. (2011). *Write to live: Telling our stories.* Bloomington, IN: iUniverse

Simpson, C. (2005). *Inside the Crips: Life inside L.A.'s most notorious gang.* New York, NY: St. Martin's Press.

Sloan, C. (Director). (2005). *Bastards of the Party* [Documentary]. United States: HBO

Tejada, D. (2010). *Trafficked.* Oakland, CA: Youth Radio. Retrieved May 7, 2013, from http://www.npr.org/2010/12/06/131757019/youth-radio-trafficked-teen-girls-describe-life-in-the-game

T'Shaka, O. (2004). *The integration trap: The generation gap caused by a choice between two cultures.* Oakland, CA: Pan African Publishers and Distributors.

United States Department of Veteran's Affairs. (2012). *Complex PTSD*. Retrieved May 7, 2013, from http://www.ptsd.va.gov/professional/pages/complex-ptsd.asp

Williams, E. (1944). *Capitalism and slavery*. Chapel Hill, NC: North Carolina Press

Young, A. (2008, March 28). Deadly silence: Stop snitching's fatal legacy. *Wiretap Magazine*. Retrieved August 16, 2013, from http://www.wiretapmag.org/race/43473/

Websites:
Motivating, Inspiring, Supporting, and Serving Sexually Exploited Youth (MISSSEY): http://www.misssey.org/
Bay Area Woman Against Rape: http://www.bawar.org/
Youth Radio: http://www.youthradio.org/
United Nations Children's Rights: http://www.unicef.org/crc/index_30177.html